Katazome

Editor: Chris Rich
Art Director: Kathleen Holmes
Production: Elaine Thompson, Kathleen Holmes, Charlie Covington
Illustrations: Charlie Covington
Photography: Evan Bracken (Light Reflections, Hendersonville, NC);
  Gary Lundgren

Published in 1993 by Lark Books
Altamont Press
50 College Street
Asheville, NC 28801
U.S.A.

© 1993, Lark Books

Library of Congress Cataloging-in-Publication Data
    Katazome : Japanese paste-resist dyeing for contemporary use /
by Kumiko Murashima.
        p.   cm.
    Includes bibliographical references and index.
    ISBN 0-937274-72-0
    1. Dyes and dyeing--Textile fibers.   2. Stencil work.
3. Textile design.   I. Title.
TT853.M87   1993
746.6--dc20   93-34626
                                                           CIP

10 9 8 7 6 5 4 3 2 1

Printed in Hong Kong by Oceanic Graphic Printing

Cover: *Detail of the stencil-dyed rice paper shown at the
bottom of page 87. Designed and executed by the author.*

Page 1: *Stencil-dyed rice paper, designed and executed by
the author.*

Page 3: *Contemporary abstract stencil pattern designed by
the author.*

Pages 4 and 5: *Stencil-dyed rice paper, created for use in a
fan. Designed by Keisuke Serizawa.*

Katazome

Japanese Paste-Resist
Dyeing for Contemporary Use

Kumiko Murashima

Lark Books

TABLE OF

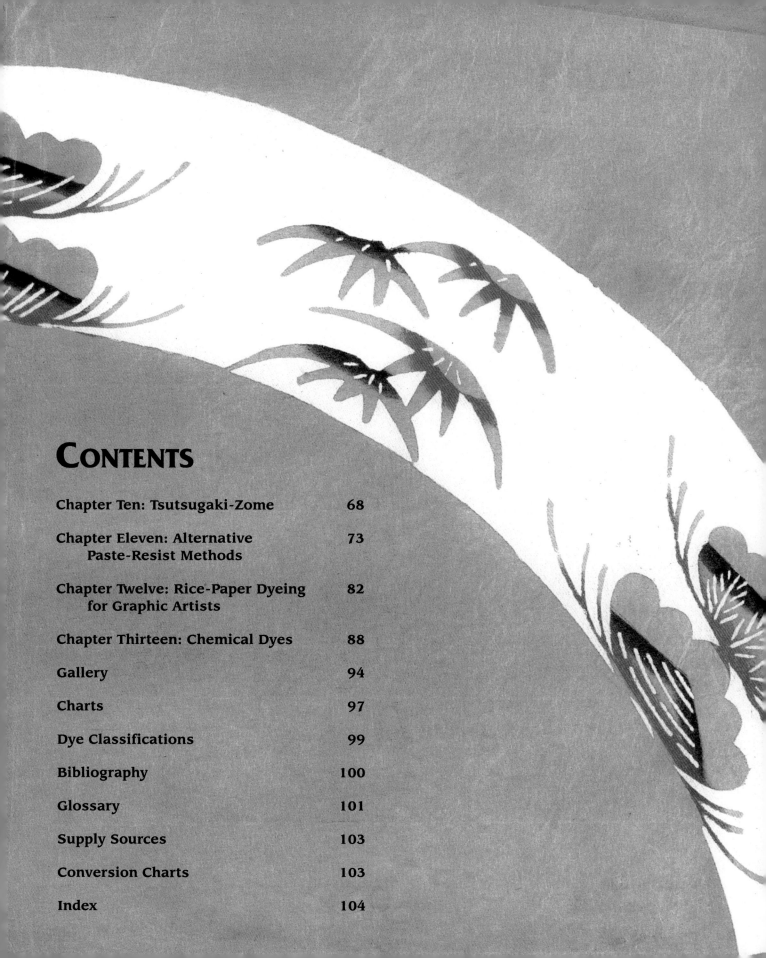

CONTENTS

ACKNOWLEDGEMENTS

This book is dedicated to Mr. Keisuke Serizawa and to my parents.

Ever since my arrival in the United States, my highest goal has been to contribute to the development of the field of dyeing. I would like to express my deep appreciation to my teacher in Japan, **Mr. Keisuke Serizawa**, who taught me the skills and gave me the encouragement necessary to achieve this goal. Until his death, Mr. Serizawa was one of Japan's fifty *Intangible Cultural Properties and National Treasures*. This honorary title, bestowed upon selected artists who represent a variety of visual arts and crafts as well as theater arts, was granted to Mr. Serizawa in recognition of his excellence in the field of dyeing crafts. Some of the photographs in this book are of pieces designed by him. I am also grateful to **Rowan College of New Jersey** for its ongoing support of my endeavors in the field of art.

Many thanks to the following people for their contributions.

Gary Lundgren, who devoted an entire summer to the book's black-and-white photography.

Mr. Tetsuo Fujimoto, Associate Professor of Art at the Seian University of Art and Design in Japan, and Fulbright Artist-in-Residence and Visiting Professor at Montclair State College (1992-1993), for the selection and loan of the photographs on pages 94, 95, and 96.

The five stencil-dyers whose works are portrayed in Mr. Fujimoto's photographs: **Yukihiko Tajima** (page 96); **Hideharu Naito** (page 95); **Syojiro Kato** (page 94); **Mihoko Ogino** (page 95); and **Keiko Kanesaki** (page 96). These distinguished artists are all residents of Kyoto, Japan.

Yunoki Samiro, whose chusen designs are shown in the photographs on pages 17 and 81.

Kiyoto Shimodaira, who designed and executed the kimono shown on page 13, executed the kimono (designed by Mr. Serizawa) on page 55, and designed and executed the tsutsugaki wall-hangings on page 70.

Valborg Fletre Linn, for having provided the Procion MX fiber-reactive dye formulas and the dye-bath recipe in Chapter Thirteen and for the Dye Classification section.

Don Wiener, Director of Technical Services for PRO Chemical & Dye, Inc., for his valuable advice and invaluable patience.

Evan Bracken, owner of Light Reflections in Hendersonville, North Carolina, who took the photographs of dyed rice paper.

Chapter One, "The History and Development of Katazome," is derived in part from the writings of **Mr. Kichiemon Okamura**, one of Japan's best known scholars in the field of Japanese folk arts and crafts.

Photographs of works not designed or executed by myself are accompanied by legends that either specify the piece's designer and maker or state that the design is a traditional one. All other designs are my own.

Kumiko Murashima
Associate Professor of Art
Department of Art
Rowan College of New Jersey
Glassboro, New Jersey

Samples of stencil-dyed wallpaper, designed by Keisuke Serizawa and executed by anonymous artisans.

8

INTRODUCTION

The author created this design on rice paper by combining the use of a stencil pattern and the tsutsugaki technique described in Chapter Ten.

The traditional Japanese art of *katazome* (paste-resist stencil dyeing) is an ancient one, yet it offers to both the present-day hobbyist and to the professional fiber or graphic artist not only an aesthetically pleasing alternative to better-known dyeing techniques but also an opportunity to expand one's knowledge of the Japanese people and their handicrafts.

The basic stencil-dyeing process is not complex. First, a stencil is cut and placed on a piece of fabric. Next, resist paste is applied through the stencil. The stencil is removed, the pasted fabric is dried in sunlight and treated with sizing, and dyes or pigments are brushed onto areas that are not protected by paste. A color fixative is applied, and finally, the fabric is soaked in water to remove the paste.

Other countries have made use of stencils and resists to dye fabrics, but on the Japanese mainland, stencil-dyeing techniques reached unparalleled levels of sophistication. And on the beautiful Okinawan Islands of Japan, basic katazome methods were adapted and further refined to produce the distinctive *bingata-zome* style. Bingata-zome, characterized by bright colors (especially scarlet), fine lines, and powerfully personal designs, is emphasized in this book because it is uniquely suited for contemporary use.

Most Japanese dyers begin by learning stencil dyeing precisely because it helps them to understand the close interaction between fabric, dye, pattern, and use, but the artist who achieves proficiency in katazome gains more than an understanding of materials or technical steps. The expert practitioner of this technique comes to understand his or her relationship to the art that he or she creates. As you learn katazome, you too will engage in this fascinating process.

This book is written for all those who would like to know more about katazome: students, industrial textile designers, print-makers, graphic artists, and teachers of fiber arts, special education, and art therapy. And last, but not least, this book is for hobbyists who would like to expand their knowledge of basic dyeing techniques.

Within these pages, you will find detailed instructions for creating your own stencil-dyed fabrics. Critical steps in the process are illustrated by means of photographs. Color photographs of completed works are also included; the unique designs they portray may inspire you as you begin to create patterns of your own. A lists of suppliers is provided, as are convenient conversion charts. The most important ingredient of this book, however, is you. If you bring with you the desire to learn and the patience to be taught, you will soon a part of the world of katazome.

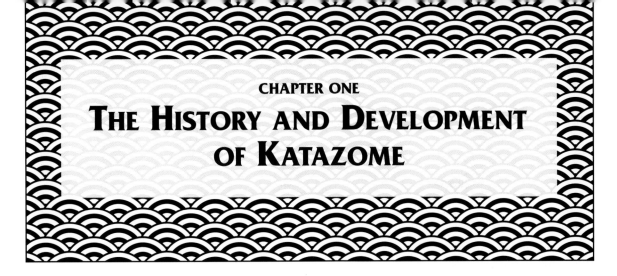

THE HISTORY AND DEVELOPMENT OF KATAZOME

Dyeing fabric probably originated with the centuries-old custom of painting the human body for ceremonial and religious purposes, a custom still practiced in some parts of the world. From this need to beautify both the body and the environment, several dyeing methods gradually developed in Oriental countries and island groups. Legend has it that fabrics were first dyed in India around 1500 B.C. Of the dyeing techniques that subsequently developed, three of the earliest known were particularly important in Japan.

The first was the *freehand* technique, which involved using one's hands to draw designs directly on fabric. As time passed, artists discovered that better designs could be created by using pieces of wood and stones as stamps. From that discovery, a more sophisticated method developed, that of *wood-block dyeing*, in which designs are carved into a wooden stamp. For obvious reasons, the aesthetic effects of wood-block dyeing are more indirect, more formal, and more organized in expression than those of freehand dyeing.

From very elementary designs, created by carving bamboo or wooden sticks, four basic approaches to the wood-block method gradually emerged. These are the *negative, positive, outlined negative,* and *outlined positive* design styles (see page 23) also used in katazome. A time-consuming technique, wood-block dyeing awaited the invention of paper for its most productive use.

A third dyeing method, the technique now known as katazome (pronounced *kah-tah-zoh-meh*), is specifically Japanese and is thought to have originated during the sixteenth-century Heian period. *Kata* means *stencil*

Traditional bingata stencil pattern, executed by the author. Shown on pages 12 and 25 are designs created with this pattern.

or *pattern. Zome* is a form of the verb *someru,* which means *to dye*—hence *katazome* (stencil dyeing).

Though the Chinese had dyed fabrics by using cut-paper stencils before, the resist that they used was created from soybeans and was a product far less versatile than the rice-based resist paste that Japanese dyers developed. And although carved wooden stamps are durable, Japanese rice-paper stencils, strengthened with persimmon juice, are not only long-lasting but are also far more easily carved and much more flexible than wood.

Ever since its invention, katazome has been widely used by Japanese professional craftsmen and dye-craft artists, who have found themselves more easily able to express themselves with this technique than with any other. Perhaps because katazome so freely permitted artistic expression, and also because Japan was a major producer of rice, the art form developed quite rapidly, within a fairly short period of time.

Specimens of the earliest katazome are rare, in part because garments, by their very nature, are short-lived, and in part because it was the Japanese custom to bury the deceased person's clothing along with his mortal remains. Existing evidence, however, suggests that the techniques used to dye Japanese fabrics four hundred years ago differed little from the techniques used today. Fragments of ancient vestments found in Shoso-In Temple, for instance, prove that many different dyeing techniques were used—batik *(roketsu-zome),* tie-dyeing *(shibori-zome),* freehand dyeing, and wooden-clump dyeing among them. It is likely that katazome was a natural outgrowth of these earlier dyeing techniques.

Many variations of katazome exist; one style—bingata-zome—developed in the lush, subtropical Okinawan Islands, where vegetation abounds and

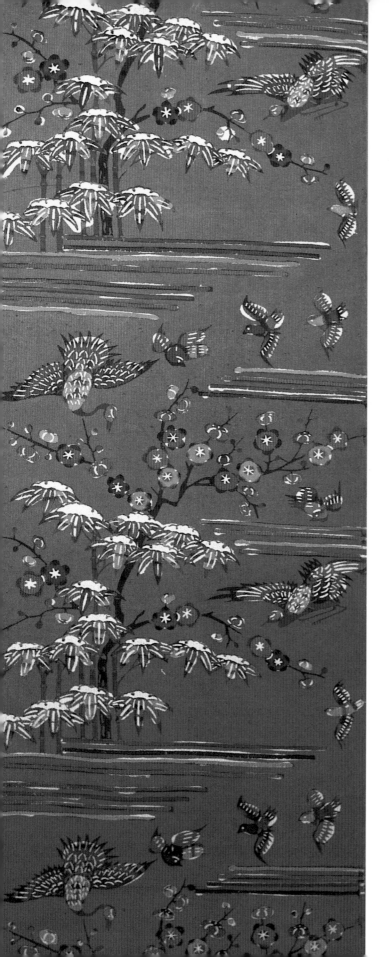

colorful flowers bloom year-round. Bingata's very name reflects its conceptual roots. The word *bin* refers not only to the color red, the predominant color used in bingata, but also to color in general. *Gata* means *pattern.* Bingata-zome therefore translates literally as *red-pattern dyeing.*

Bingata-zome is sometimes thought to have originated with batik, the wax-resist dyeing technique in widespread use throughout the South Pacific. Certainly, both batik and bingata make use of abundant color. The techniques, the raw materials, and the terminology involved in each, however, are sufficiently different to justify classifying the latter as among the family of dyed fabrics originating in the main islands of Japan; bingata-zome was most likely a direct outgrowth of mainland Japanese katazome. It subsequently developed independently, evolving in ways that suited it to the subtropical climate of the islands where it was practiced.

In its present-day dyeing techniques, Japan is one of the most progressive countries in the world—aesthetically, technically, and conceptually. In fact, it is difficult to imagine a Japanese culture without dyed fabrics, many types of which are produced for traditional Japanese costumes (the *kimono* and *obi*) and for decorative items as well. Certainly, dyeing is one of Japan's foremost cultural accomplishments.

The Japanese artisans who practice katazome fall into three main classifications: those who faithfully follow traditional dyeing techniques; artists who meet contemporary market demands by creating textile designs for machine-dyed and mass-produced fabrics; and those who develop and practice their own individual dyeing styles and expressions. In spite of the diverse goals and activities of these three groups, however, respect and collaboration are prevalent. A work is not judged on the basis of its artist's choice of approach, but on its quality, which is defined in terms of professional standards set within each individual approach.

Though the various stages of katazome were once treated as individual specialties (stencil cutting, for example, was a separate craft), in an artistic context, when a single person completes every step of the stencil-dyeing process, the results are likely to be far more pleasing aesthetically. And the contemporary dyer or graphic artist who learns every step of katazome not only learns all there is to know about traditional Japanese stencil dyeing but will discover new paths to creativity as well.

Opposite page:
The stencil on page 10 was used to dye this obi (or Japanese belt).

Right: Stencil-dyed kimono. Traditional design executed by Kiyoto Shimodaira, who used pigments and indigo blue.

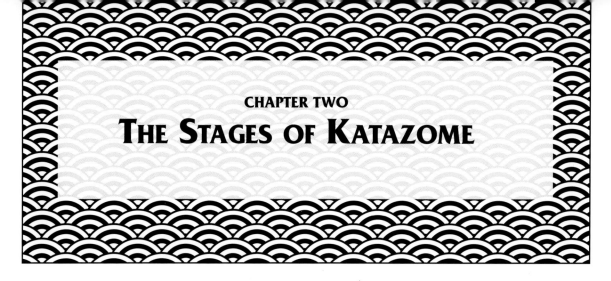

CHAPTER TWO
THE STAGES OF KATAZOME

Katazome is a paradoxical art form. On the one hand, this dyeing technique offers unparalleled freedom of expression. On the other hand, its execution is quite restrictive; steps must be followed in sequence, and the timing of these steps requires care.

There are two basic techniques in paste-resist dyeing: katazome (the stencil-dyeing process) and *tsutsuga-ki-zome* (the tube-drawing process). The first is executed with a paper stencil. In the second, the resist is applied freehand with a paper cone that resembles a cake-decorating tool.

The separate stages of basic katazome and of tsutsugaki-zome execution are not complex, but beginners may find the sequence of steps somewhat confusing. First, take a good look at the outline provided for basic katazome. The tsutsugaki steps are similar, but no stencil is required.

Basic Katazome

- Select and pre-treat your fabric
- Design, cut, and reinforce a stencil
- Prepare the resist paste
- Prepare a paste-laying board
- Position the fabric on the paste-laying board
- Apply the resist paste to the fabric through the stencil paper
- Remove the stencil paper
- Dry the fabric by suspending it on *harite* (wooden stretchers) and securing *shinshi* (bamboo stretchers) to its back
- Apply soybean-juice sizing to the fabric
- Prepare and apply the dye or pigment
- If necessary, steam and apply a color fixative
- Soak the fabric in water to remove the paste *(mizumoto)*
- Dry the fabric

Variations

Paste-resist dyeing has many variations, each of which is covered in subsequent chapters. Pigments and dyes, for example, can be applied in different sequences. And paste-resist application techniques are numerous. Following are brief descriptions of these methods; don't let yourself be intimidated by them! Though they may seem confusing at first, they represent a wealth of creative possibility.

The **conventional katazome dye-application method** (see Chapter Nine) consists of three stages:

First, detail colors are applied to portions of the areas not covered by paste; this process is known as *irosashi. Gradation coloring* may also be added to irosashi areas.

Then *fusenori* is executed; the irosashi areas are protected with paste.

Finally, the remaining design areas are dyed with a background (or base) color.

Several **variations on the conventional dyeing method** are also possible:

In one variation, the background (all areas not protected by paste) is dyed, usually with a light color. Then detail colors are applied on top of the background color, using colors that will blend well with the dyed background.

Another method, *sashi-wake,* calls for filling in all paste-free areas, using a small brush and multiple colors. No background color is applied.

In a third variation, known as *atosashi* (or final touch), either the detail colors alone or both detail and background colors are refined after they've been applied. A transparent pigment or dye is used for this purpose.

The fourth variation calls for dyeing only a background color. One popular version of this method is *aizome* (indigo vat dyeing).

Resist-paste can be used and applied in different ways (see Chapters Ten and Eleven):

The most frequently used method of freehand paste application, in which no stencil is used at all, is tsutsuga-ki-zome. In this method, the paste is squeezed out through a conical tube (or *tsutsu).*

It's also possible to apply paste using nothing more than your hand or a spatula. Neither a stencil nor a conical tube is required.

The paste itself can be colored. Dyeing with colored paste (or *ironori*) is known as *nazome.*

Instead of applying the paste through a stencil, it can also be stamped onto the fabric with carved wood-blocks. Colored paste is sometimes used with this technique.

In addition, **techniques** can be combined:

Katazome and tsutsugaki-zome work well together.

Either katazome or tsutsugaki-zome can be executed along with tie-dyeing *(shibori-zome).*

In one especially sophisticated technique, *tsujigahana,* three methods are combined: katazome or tsutsuga-ki, shibori, and fine embroidery.

Even **stencils** can be used in different ways:

In the *kasane* technique, one or more stencils are overlapped on a single piece of fabric.

And in *chusen-zome,* a simple mass-production process, designs are repeated by attaching the stencil to a hinged frame, which is lowered over sections of the fabric.

CHAPTER THREE
THE FABRIC

Selecting the Fabric

Your choice of fabric will depend in part on the pattern you have designed. For intricate, finely-detailed patterns, select tight weaves; for patterns with large shapes, choose fabrics that are relatively loose in structure. The more open the weave of the fabric, the richer the dyed colors will be.

Use only natural fibers, either protein or cellulose. Those that follow are all suitable for stencil dyeing; the easiest with which to work are cotton, linen, silk, and wool.

Cellulose Fibers
Cotton
Linen
Jute
Ramie
Hemp
Sisal
Rayon

Protein Fibers
Wool (including cashmere
   and other specialty wools)
Silk
Alpaca
Mohair
Angora

Left: Full Moon in Indigo Blue. *Stencil-dyed yardage fabric.*

Opposite page, top and bottom: *Stencil-dyed yardage fabric, designed and executed by Yunoki Samiro. The artist used the chusen-zome method described in Chapter Eleven.*

Pre-Treating the Fabric

To dye fabric successfully, any starch, sizing, and grease in the material must be removed in a process known as *scouring*. Fabrics that are easily penetrated by dye can simply be soaked in warm water, but others may need to be soaked in hot water or even boiled. Those that come straight from the factory (sometimes known as *grey goods*) often contain substances that lead to streaking during the dyeing process. Immersion dyeing may disguise these impurities, but because less dye is applied in katazome, cleaning the fabric is especially important.

Cottons and linens that aren't excessively starched or sized are scoured by boiling. First, fold the fabric into the smallest sections possible; make accordion folds, first in one direction and then in the other. Fill a very large enamel pot with water, to within 10" or 12" (25.4 or 30.5 cm) from the top; use approximately one gallon (3.78 l) of water for each yard (91.4 cm) of material. Bring the water to a boil, place the folded fabric into it, and boil (uncovered) for 30 to 40 minutes. Hang the fabric to cool in the open air for at least 30 minutes, and then rinse it out under a running faucet (not in a container) in order to remove

the starch completely. It's especially important that the fabric be cool before you take this step. Finally, hang the fabric straight up and down on a clothesline to dry.

Heavily starched or sized cottons may require slightly different treatment. First, weigh the fabric. Next, soak it in warm water for one hour. Then prepare a solution of washing soda (sodium carbonate; 6% of the fabric's weight), mild detergent (1% of the fabric's weight), and water (1 gal. or 3.78 liters for each yard or 91.44 cm of fabric) in a large enamel pot. Bring the water to a boil, submerge the fabric, and boil uncovered for 40 to 50 minutes. Hang the fabric to cool, rinse it thoroughly, and hang it again to dry.

Some linens can be scoured in the same way as heavily starched cottons, but the rather hard fiber structures of stiff, starch-laden, sized linens and some coarse silks need to be softened in a chemical solution. The Japanese name for this process of refinement is *neru*.

You may fold linens for this process, but don't fold silks, which are too fragile. First, pre-soak and then drain the fabric. Calculate 3%-4% of the fabric's weight, and then add that amount of potassium carbonate to a large pot of cold water, using the same water-to-fabric ratio given earlier in this section. Bring the solution to a boil before submerging the

fabric in it. Boil for about 30 minutes, stirring period-ically with a stick. Cool the fabric in the open air, rinse it thoroughly under running water, and hang it on a line to dry. Be sure not to wring linens or silks, or you'll end up with unsightly wrinkles.

Fragile silks and wools should not be boiled. Instead, soak the fabric for 30 to 40 minutes in 158° F to 176° F (70° C to 80° C) water; don't fold the material. Allow the fabric to cool down in the water, rinse in lukewarm, running water, and dry. Raw silks are scoured for the same amount of time in a solution of 3% washing soda and 3% mild detergent. Keep the solution's temperature at 194° F to 212° F (90° C to 100° C). Cool the fabric in the open air, and then rinse it well before drying.

To dry a very long piece of fabric, attach harite (wooden stretchers) to each short end, and then attach the harite (in full sunshine) to two trees or two vertical poles. Be sure to stretch the fabric so that it is held flat and level to the ground. Attach shinshi (bamboo stretchers) across the fabric's back, 4" to 6" (10.2 to 15.2 cm) apart. Harite are unnecessary for smaller pieces of fabric. Instead, stretch these on two shinshi, running each one diagonally from opposite corners of the fabric. Tie a rope to the point where the shinshi intersect, and suspend the fabric so that it is level to the ground. (Harite and shinshi are pic-tured on pages 43 and 44.)

Once your fabric has been cleaned and dried, mea-sure and record its weight. You may need this mea-surement to calculate dye quantities.

Stencil-dyed paper place mat, designed by Keisuke Serizawa and executed by unknown artisans.

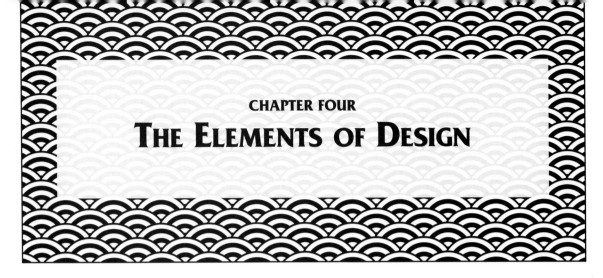

CHAPTER FOUR

THE ELEMENTS OF DESIGN

Katazome, by its very nature, implies certain design restrictions. Don't let the word *restriction,* however, strike you as pejorative. For the Japanese artist, the constraints imposed by katazome are precisely what produces its greatest rewards. Indeed, the Japanese artist knows that embracing and observing the boundaries that these constraints impose will result in aesthetically interesting design work.

Unless the restrictions inherent in working with stencil paper make it technically impossible to execute your particular design ideas, you shouldn't neglect any of them. Although the work you produce in an attempt to break free of these limitations may demonstrate technical skill, it won't make a strong design statement.

The next chapter gives specific instructions for drawing patterns and carving stencils. Before you begin, consider the katazome design concepts that follow.

And keep in mind as you read this chapter that a finished, repeated design on fabric shouldn't be compared with the purely graphic, conceptually independent, and non-repeated design on paper; the two will never be exactly the same.

Types of Patterns

Individual Unit Patterns and Continuous Unit Patterns

An *individual unit pattern* is recognizable as a design that is complete in itself. It does not blend into other patterns; it is completely independent, its borders are discrete, and it is not repeated on the fabric. A *continuous unit pattern*, on the other hand, repeats itself in either two (vertical or horizontal) directions or in four (vertical and horizontal) directions. The purpose and character of the finished product should be con-

Continuous unit stencil pattern. Its traditional karakusa design is characterized by swirling lines and a floral motif.

sidered as you decide how to lay out a continuous unit pattern.

Symmetrical and Asymmetrical Patterns

Patterns are either symmetrical or asymmetrical. A symmetrical individual unit pattern consists of divisions, each of equal size. An asymmetrical individual unit pattern has neither a center line and point, nor any equally-sized divisions within it. Complicated placement or distorted pattern shapes may disguise center lines and points, but when they exist, the pattern is still considered to be symmetrical.

One good example of an asymmetrical pattern is found in the *Eba* style. In this technique, the fabric for a kimono is temporarily sewn together in its finished shape. A design is then either drawn on it freehand with resist paste, using the tsutsugaki-zome tube described in Chapter Ten, or created with a stencil pattern. This style's unique characteristic is its unbalanced balance; its irregularity and the looseness of its background create an aesthetic quality that is very relaxed and unrestricted. Eba patterns frequently feature landscapes.

The Japanese love nature, and nature is characteristically asymmetrical in its forms. Japanese gardens, for instance, are designed to emphasize that which is unbalanced rather than that which is equal and balanced.

Realistic and Abstract Patterns

Arguments in favor of either abstract or realistic designs in stencil dyeing are frequent and often unnecessary. Understand these different design concepts, by all means, but avoid value judgements of either.

Abstract design, unlike realistic design, simply isn't related to easily recognizable, familiar forms. In fact, it attempts to express its aesthetic qualities without allowing its audience to recognize the objects or shapes that it uses. You might think, therefore, that these two design types are entirely opposed to one another, but this is not so. The abstract often starts out as the realistic; when it doesn't, it's seldom successful and will seem to be missing something important. The abstract can be created by abbreviating and emphasizing one area of the realistic and by repeating these abbreviations and emphases several times.

At a certain stage of design, once you're familiar with the basic elements, you're likely to find that you are unconsciously creating abstract designs, without intending to do so. Making distinctions between abstract and realistic approaches will seem insignificant. Until—and even after—you reach that point, remember that it is you—and not a theory—that brings your designs alive and gifts them with originality.

Opposite page:
Contemporary
abstract on rice paper.
Note that this design
was created with the
stencil pattern shown
on page 3.

Right: Kimono dyed
with pigment and
indigo blue. Tradi-
tional karakusa
design.

Traditional Patterns

Traditional designs are based on design concepts that have accumulated over a long period of time; they're named after different periods or people. Their close association with actual people and the particular lifestyles of historical periods lend to many of these designs a warm and intimate tone. They often make use of bold repetitions. Certain kinds of traditional patterns repeat themselves in katazome and its variations.

Among these traditional design styles are *komon,* one consisting of very small, scattered design elements, and *karakusa,* with its swirling, curved lines or floral designs combined with swirling lines, on a blue or dark green background. Bingata is another type of traditional design style; it is characterized by its red or scarlet flowers combined with yellow, green, magenta, and indigo blue scenery or scenic elements such as streams, butterflies, pine trees, birds, clouds, flowers, willow trees, and bamboos. These elements can either be arranged in a specific order or placed randomly. In some instances, they're scattered in a wide, open space; in others, the small shapes are clustered close together.

Even in similar design motifs, there are many different approaches to design in terms of how objects are interpreted. The same design elements can be delicate, free and cheerful, formal, or dynamic in expression. But one thing can be said of all the traditional katazome approaches to design: while they are all bright and colorful, they retain an aura of subtlety and peace that any era and any generation can appreciate.

Sometimes it's helpful to copy traditional designs for purposes of study. Understanding the various features of these designs will enhance your own approach to stencil designing. Your copies needn't be exact; for the beginner, copying details isn't as important as learning basic styles. It's also worthwhile to know why and how a given design was established within the social and cultural background of its time and place.

The distinguishing features of both traditional and contemporary katazome designs are a function of the resist paste with which they are created. It just isn't possible to recreate these features with any other fabric-dyeing method. While tie-dyeing, for example, offers spontaneous enjoyment, its effects are directly related to the effects of the threads or cords that are used for its execution. Batik design is defined by the results of the wax application that creates the crackled background or design areas; while batik has its spontaneous design aspects, its designs are distinctly different from those of paste-resist dyeing. And in silk screening, only certain types of coloring agents can be used. Silk-screened colors can never measure up to the quality of resist-paste colors, which penetrate the fabric thoroughly and deeply.

Though the kind of design that you eventually create will naturally reflect both your own lifestyle and your own philosophy, one of the most important things that you must do when you first learn to design is to approach existing designs with an open yet faithful mind. Respect traditional designs, and attempt to understand both how they've been created and the sources from which they've been brought forth.

A continuous unit stencil pattern that illustrates the karakusa style (swirling lines and floral motifs).

Design Types

Four basic design types are used in katazome, each of which can be used by itself or in combination with one of the others.

Negative Designs *(Hinata)*

A negative design is one in which the figure sections are cut out of the paper stencil. When resist paste is applied over the stencil, the paste sets onto the fabric through the cut-out holes so that undyed (negative) figures are backed by a colored ground.

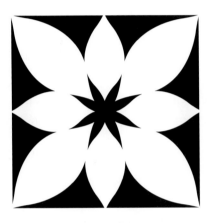

Positive Designs *(Kage)*

Positive designs consist of colored figures on the fabric. The background (rather than the figures) is cut from the stencil paper. The dyeing process leaves an undyed ground with colored (positive) figures on it.

Outlined Positive Designs *(Hinata-no-kukuri)*

Outlined positive designs are comprised of colored (positive) figures, surrounded by thin, undyed (negative) lines which have been cut out on the stencil paper. The cut-out areas in the stencil pattern permit resist paste to protect the fabric that is exposed through them. The designs on the finished fabric therefore show undyed outlines around dyed figures.

Outlined Negative Designs *(Kage-no-kukuri)*

Outlined negative designs have white (negative) figures which are surrounded by thin, colored (positive) lines. Figures are cut from the stencil pattern; the thin outlines remain as uncut portions of the paper. Because these thin stencil lines prevent the fabric from being protected by resist paste, the outlines that result are subsequently colored with dye or pigment.

For a beginner, one of the key aspects of design is learning to visualize the areas of your design that will eventually be cut away—learning, in other words, to see its positive and negative aspects.

Joints *(Tsunagi)*

In katazome, floating elements of designs, the backgrounds of which will be cut away, must somehow be attached to the rest of the stencil or the stencil will fall apart. *Joints*—narrow strips of paper that are left uncut—serve to hold these floating elements together. In outlined positive and outlined negative designs, for example, joints are a technical necessity. They provide an excellent example, however, of a restriction that can serve an aesthetic as well as a practical purpose. While it is possible to cut joints out after the stencil is reinforced with silk gauze (see pages 31–32), you may prefer to incorporate them into the design itself; they can lend it a special keenness and intensity.

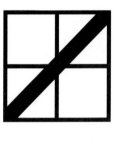 

Registration Marks

All designs are limited in length and width by the length and width of the fabric to be dyed. When you're repeating a pattern along a length of fabric, it's therefore especially important to match the sides of each repeated design unit. After you've applied resist paste through the stencil, you'll lift the stencil up and replace it next to the first pasted area in order to continue the pattern; the stencil must be carefully re-positioned each time so that no gaps or overlaps exist between one dyed instance of the pattern and another.

To help guide you during this process, *registration marks* are cut on the stencil. By looking through the marks on the stencil and lining them up with the paste-covered marks on the fabric, you'll be able to match each design unit exactly. The next chapter includes directions for cutting these marks.

Left: *The top three figures in the left-hand column represent stencil patterns with joints. These joints serve to hold the stencil together until a sheet of silk gauze has been attached to it. Once the gauze is in place, the joints can be cut away, as shown in the figures in the right-hand column. Joints are not always cut on patterns; see the fourth figure in each column.*

Opposite page: *Traditional Okinawan design executed on rice paper. The stencil pattern with which this was created is shown on page 10.*

CHAPTER FIVE
THE STENCIL

Because the carved stencil determines whether or not the finished design will be successful, the paper from which it's made needs to be thin enough to cut, yet strong, flexible, and long-lasting, too. *Katagami,* the durable stencil paper with which katazome is executed, satisfies all these requirements. It is made from laminated layers of handmade rice paper and is strengthened with the juice of unripe persimmons. The laminated sheets are dried in the sun and then smoked for ten days. Tannin in the juice and resin in the sawdust smoke strengthen the paper and make it waterproof.

Katagami is available in various sizes, thicknesses, and weights. For most purposes, pieces measuring about 21" x 35" (53.3 x 88.9 cm) are suitable. Select a paper that is closest in thickness to the thickness of your fabric (No. 10 for fine silks, No. 12 for most cottons, and No. 14 for very coarse materials). If you're unable to find katagami, you can use the opaque paper sold as stencil paper in art-supply stores, but it won't last as long.

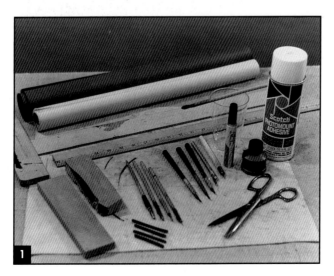
1

Photo 1 shows the items you'll need in order to sketch and cut your stencil: a sheet of katagami, a sheet of tracing paper, a sheet of vinyl about 1/8" to 1/4" (.3 to .6 cm) thick, an assortment of knives and blades (or a craft knife), temporary spray adhesive (the same type of adhesive in stick form is even easier to use), a ruler, a soft pencil or a pen and India ink, a few charcoal pencils, one rough and one smooth whetstone (necessary if you're using traditional knives), a felt-tipped pen, a small plastic cup, a pair of scissors, and a bamboo brush.

Designing the Pattern

Once you've gathered your supplies, make a rough sketch of your design on a piece of paper, using charcoal or a soft pencil. Several facts must be kept in mind as you do so. First, you'll need to study your fabric and determine the size of the design area. Though the design you carve on your stencil should be exactly that size, the actual piece of stencil paper should be somewhat larger; the uncarved borders will protect surrounding fabric areas from resist paste.

As you sketch your design, also remember that if you intend to repeat that design on your fabric, you'll need to make sure that opposing sides of the stencil will match each other when the pattern is repeated. Creating a carefully matched design, one in which, for example, the tip of a leaf appears on one side and the remainder of the leaf on the other, will help; cutting registration marks will also prove useful.

If you plan to continue the pattern in only two directions, marks should be drawn (and subsequently cut) on each of the appropriate two pattern sides. If you intend to repeat the pattern in four directions, registration marks should be cut on all four sides. To place them correctly, first imagine a border about

1/8" to 1/4" (.3 to .6 cm) wide, just around the design area. Next, decide which of the four design sides will need to be matched in order to repeat your design.

On each of the selected two or four sides, sketch two, small triangular marks within the narrow border. Be sure that each set of two marks is exactly aligned with the set on the opposite side of the stencil. (Each mark should be equidistant from the corner of the design that is nearest to it.) When you lift and replace the stencil, you'll overlap the registration marks on the stencil with the paste-covered marks on the fabric.

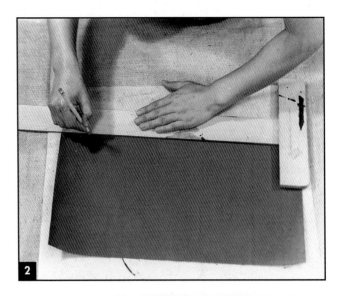

After you've sketched your preliminary design, you'll need to mark the borders of the design area on the stencil paper (Photo 2). Purchased stencil paper usually comes rolled up; its face side is smooth and is on the inside of the roll. Use a pencil and a square or triangle to draw the border lines on the face side of the stencil paper, making sure that the corners are square and that the marked design area is centered. Leave an additional 2" to 2-1/2" (5.1 to 6.4 cm) *fuchiba* (or border) around the edge of the design area. This border will protect the fabric around the design area from paste which might otherwise spread beyond the edges of the carved stencil. It will also keep your pattern in good condition. Mark the border clearly with a felt-tipped pen (Photo 3).

Trace your sketched design onto a sheet of tracing paper, using a narrow, felt-tipped pen or a brush and India ink (Photo 4). Be sure that the tracing paper is thin enough to see through. Thin paper will also make carving the stencil easier, as you'll be cutting through both the tracing and the stencil paper underneath it. Japanese artists use a paper known as *minogami;* thin commercial tracing paper makes a good substitute.

Next, place the tracing onto the face of the stencil paper. Be sure to align it correctly. Then fill in any border areas between the edges of your design area and the marked outline on the stencil paper (Photo 5). Remove the tracing when you're finished.

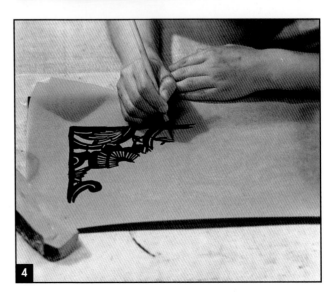

Coat the stencil with a temporary adhesive that comes in stick form (a product now available in many art-supply stores) or with temporary spray adhesive or very soft beeswax. Then carefully press the tracing paper onto the stencil paper (Photo 6) so that the two adhere to each other. Rub the tracing paper gently but thoroughly with your hands to eliminate all wrinkles from its surface and all air bubbles from underneath it. For small wrinkles and bubbles, use your fingernails. Check for any white, bumpy areas; if you

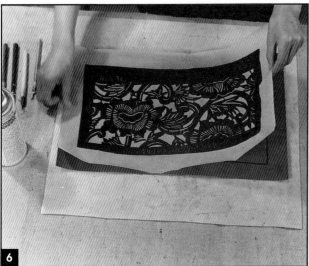

find any, you may need to lift the tracing paper up and rub off the excess adhesive or wax in those spots with a fingernail or clean paper towel.

Finally, you'll need to carve the design through both layers of paper, following the pattern lines on the tracing paper.

Carving the Stencil

Stencils can be carved with craft knives; these are readily available and come with replaceable blades. If you'd rather follow in the steps of Japanese stencil-cutting artists, you'll need to order one or more traditional knives instead; they're available with round, hollow blades and with straight blades. (Komon designs, consisting of extremely small patterns, are typically carved with these special blades and with punches.)

The traditional knife (Photo 7) must be sharpened frequently. Place the blade's edge evenly on a whetstone, holding your forefinger on its top, flat surface. Use your other fingers and thumb to grasp the handle as you push the blade back and forth. Concentrate your energy in your wrist, keep the blade at an angle of 18° to 22°, and apply even pressure as you work. (Excessive pressure may cause the blade to break, so do be careful.) Apply an even, smooth, steady pressure along the length of the blade—and don't forget to sharpen both edges.

Place the stencil and tracing paper on a vinyl board or on a self-healing, reversible cutting mat, available at many art-supply stores. Photos 8-12 illustrate the cutting process. Cut the smallest, most detailed portions first. If you start with the larger, less complex sections, you'll find that by the time you're ready to cut the delicate parts, there won't be enough uncut paper left to keep the stencil stable. When possible, work from the center of the pattern outward. Hold your blade at a 45° angle, and pull it toward you as you cut. Do be careful not to cut away the joints, or your pattern will fall apart.

As you cut, grasp the handle with your thumb and forefinger, resting the handle against the side of your third finger. Keep the paper steady by resting the fourth and little fingers lightly against it at a 45° angle. If you exert too much pressure on the blade as you carve, the blade will either to cut too deeply into the board or will break.

Make design changes as you cut, by all means, even if

you are copying a traditional pattern for practice. As long as you have the knife in your hand, it's not too late to alter the design. As you cut, though, remember that your final dyed pattern will be the exact size of the pattern that you carve.

After you've carved the pattern, examine it carefully from both sides; search for areas that you may have forgotten to cut. If you don't like the pattern that you've just created, stop while you're ahead! Go back and carve another. Your pattern is the basis of your finished work; if you aren't pleased with it now, you're bound to be disappointed with the final results.

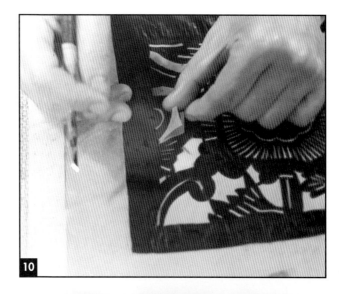

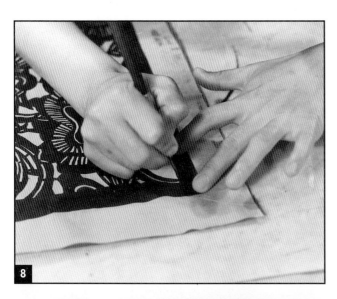

Carefully peel off the tracing paper (Photo 13). You may need to make corrections after doing so (Photo 14). Then move the stencil to a work surface.

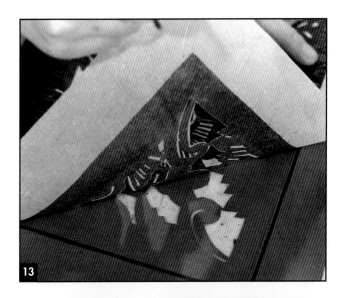

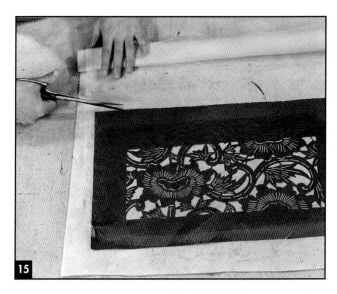

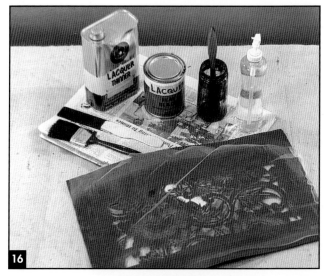

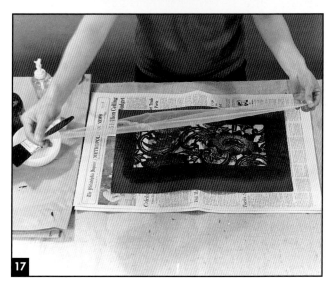

Attaching Silk Gauze to the Carved Stencil

Before you can remove the joints, you'll need to reinforce the stencil by stretching silk gauze over it. First, cut a piece of gauze just slightly larger than the stencil (Photo 15). To attach this gauze, you'll need a can of flat, black lacquer, some lacquer thinner, a small jar, a fairly stiff 2" to 2-1/2" (5.1 to 6.4 cm) paintbrush, a sprayer, some newspaper, and a wooden stirring stick (Photo 16).

Now place the stencil on several sheets of newspaper. Stretch the gauze in the direction of its warp by grasping it at diagonally opposite corners and pulling firmly (Photo 17). Avoid stretching in the weft direction! Stretch the gauze twice, once from each set of corners. Check to be certain that the woven mesh of the gauze remains square as you work; the warp and weft threads must remain perpendicular to one another.

Then place the gauze on top of the stencil, and spray it with an even coat of water to keep it in place. Examine the gauze to make sure that it is straight, and adjust it if necessary (Photo 18). Place a couple of sheets of newspaper on top of the damp gauze, and cover the newspapers with a board or with several heavy books (Photo 19). Leave the weights in place for at least 15 minutes, until the gauze is almost dry. Then remove the board (or books) and newspapers; the stencil and gauze should be barely damp.

To attach the gauze securely to the stencil, first make a mixture of two-thirds black lacquer and one-third lacquer thinner. Apply four strokes of the mixture over the gauze. Dip your paintbrush into the lacquer mixture, and shake the brush slightly to remove excess liquid. Make two diagonal brush strokes first, in an X shape; then stroke once vertically and once horizontally over the X (Photo 20).

Next, brush lacquer over the entire piece, working in the gauze's warp direction, using diagonal strokes and stroking outward at all times. Don't exert a lot of pressure with the brush. As soon as you've finished, while the gauze is still damp, clear any clogged areas in the gauze by moving a fine-tipped brush rapidly back and forth across its surface.

Before the lacquer has dried, use scissors to cut away the excess gauze along the edges of the stencil. Then turn the stencil so that the gauze faces down, and while the gauze is still damp, cut and remove the major joints, which should not yet have stuck to the

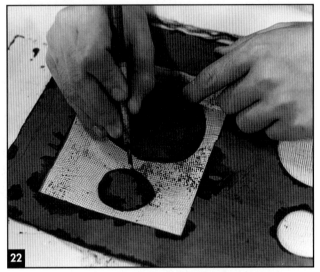

lacquered gauze. (The smaller joints should be cut last.) If you wait too long, the gauze will dry, and the joints will stick too tightly to remove; it's crucial that you work as quickly as possible. In Photos 21, 22, and 23, joint removal is demonstrated on a simple pattern. Be careful not to slice through the gauze as you cut the joints; cut the stencil lightly, just above the layer of gauze. Then lift the severed joints up by piercing them with the point of your knife blade.

The sections of gauze mesh that are not backed by paper must be completely open. Resist paste won't go through mesh that is covered with a film of lacquer, and the result will be holes in your dyed fabric's design. Examine the gauze carefully to make sure that none of the residual lacquer, which is transparent, remains. If the lacquer has become too hard to remove with a brush, try picking it out carefully with a knife blade, but be careful not to disturb or cut through the gauze threads. Blowing sharply with your mouth will also help.

Never use spray lacquer instead of liquid black lacquer from the can; it's extremely difficult to remove from the gauze mesh. The rapid brush motions that so effectively clean gauze clogged with brush-applied lacquer just won't work on sprayed lacquer. If you have trouble finding lacquer in a can, try an auto supply shop. In a pinch, you can even use polyurethane, though it takes a long time to dry and tends to be sticky.

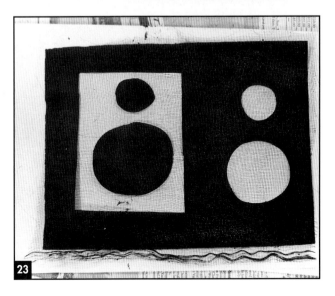

CHAPTER SIX

THE RESIST PASTE

The novice dyer may think that color application is the most important facet of design, but in many dyeing techniques, the design depends as much or more on the need to resist colors as on the need to apply them. Methods of protecting certain areas of the fabric from dye differ from technique to technique; thread is used in tie-dyeing, wax is used in batik, and in katazome, penetration of the dye or pigment is prevented with *sweet-rice resist paste.*

This resist is fine enough to permit the transfer of extremely delicate lines but is also hardy enough to serve its main purpose—dye-resistance. The somewhat elastic paste clings well to the surface of either fabric or paper, rather than soaking in. Once it has dried, it is durable enough to prevent dye from penetrating through to the fabric, yet it can be removed by soaking the fabric in water.

24

Making the Resist Paste

To make the resist paste, you'll need the items pictured in Photo 24: a clam or lobster steamer, an enamel canner, or a large, enamel, two-part steaming pot; a piece of cotton cloth (shown draped over the steamer); two mixing bowls; a sieve; a glass measuring cup; fine-grained rice bran *(komon-nuka)*; sweet-rice flour *(mochiko)*; slaked lime (calcium hydroxide); common salt; and (not shown) a wooden pestle or a stick with rounded edges.

The paste's two main ingredients are a sweet-rice (glutinous) flour, known as mochiko, which dissolves easily in water, and an especially fine-grained sweet-rice bran (komon-nuka), which is added to minimize the stickiness that the flour gives to the paste. The proportions in which you mix the bran and flour will depend on the type of fabric you're using and on your design. Fine design areas and tightly woven fabrics require a thinner paste than large design areas and loosely woven fabrics. The standard proportions of bran to flour are 6:4, 5:3, and 5:6.

In Japan, each mixture has its own name. *Nebai-nori,* or sticky paste, has a high proportion of flour and is used for fine-lined designs. *Karu-nori* (or *sakui-nori*)—ordinary paste—has a lower proportion of flour than nebai-nori does and gives a softer, vaguer look. Plan on using about two cups (240 g or 465 ml) of paste for each yard (91.44 cm) of fabric.

If komon-nuka is too costly for your budget to bear, then you may substitute the regular rice flour or polish that's available in some health-food stores for some portion of this fine-grained bran. Two alternative recipes for the paste are possible. You may mix one part komon-nuka, one part sweet-rice flour, and two parts of either regular rice flour or rice polish, or you may mix one part komon-nuka, one part sweet-

rice flour, one part rye flour, and one part regular rice flour or rice polish. But whichever recipe you use, make sure that it includes at least 25% komon-nuka. Without sufficient komon-nuka, your paste won't turn yellow enough to be clearly visible once it has been applied to the fabric, and accurate registration when repeating designs will be difficult. Also, never use wheat flour; it will soak through the fabric instead of staying on its surface.

To make the paste, first place the bran into a bowl (Photo 25). Then add the sweet-rice flour (Photo 26), and mix the two thoroughly with one hand (Photo 27). Next, sift the flour and bran together at least three times to remove any lumps.

Add lukewarm water, a little at a time, as if you were mixing cookie ingredients; knead the mixture well as you do (Photos 28-30). Stop kneading when the mixture retains its shape and feels a bit like your own earlobe (Photo 31). If the dough sticks to your hands, it's too moist or soft. The finished dough should be similar to bread dough, which retains its solid shape when it's the correct consistency.

Divide the dough into two or three sections of equal size, and shape these into doughnuts (Photo 32). Line the bottom of the steamer's upper section with wet combed-cotton cloth, place the doughnuts on the cloth (Photo 33), and then cover them with it. Assemble the steamer, cover it with a piece of clean towel, and place the lid on top of the towel. Steam the doughnuts for 30 to 40 minutes, depending on the quantity of dough. (The steamed paste is known as *mushi-nori*.) If you should need to replenish the water in the steamer, don't expose the doughnuts to air, as their surfaces will harden if you do.

While the doughnuts are still hot, turn them out into a bowl (Photo 34), and mash them immediately with

a smooth, wooden, round-edged stick or pestle (Photo 35) or with a potato masher. As you mash and mix, gradually add small amounts of hot water from the steamer (Photo 36). Work as quickly as possible. The paste must be completed before the dough has cooled, or it will become lumpy. Speed is of the essence here! Continue to add hot water, using an electric or hand beater (Photo 37) to blend the dough; mix until the dough is very smooth.

When the dough is partially mixed, measure out about one-eighth as much slaked lime as the total amount of rice flour and bran in your mixture. Place the slaked lime into the hot water remaining in the steamer (Photo 38), and stir it in well. Then wait until it settles (Photo 39). (If the water is boiling when you mix the lime into it, you needn't wait until the lime settles; just pour it in, stir it, and use it.) This solution will add body to the paste, make it more dye-resistant, and prolong its life.

Next, pour the top portion of the solution into the dough (Photo 40), a little at a time, mixing it in with a beater until the paste becomes a rich amber color (or golden yellow). As soon as the paste turns this color, stop adding the solution. Adding too much lime solution will make the paste rubbery and unusable, so if the paste turns golden yellow but still isn't soft enough, add plain boiling water instead, until the paste is smooth and elastic (Photo 41). Never mix the lime directly into the paste, or it will make the dough

lumpy. And note that the lime's effectiveness will depend on the extent to which it has been exposed to air and on its age.

Just before you reach the final stage, add about as much common salt solution to the dough as you added lime solution, dissolving the salt in a little water first and mixing it in well. Salt helps the paste to retain its moisture and smoothness. Exact proportions can't be given; you'll need twice as much in the winter, when the weather is dry, as you will in the summer. To store the dough, cover it with a damp, combed-cotton cloth, or pour water over the paste in its container.

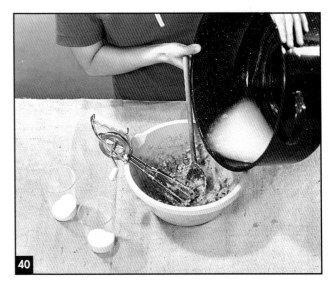

Preparing the Paste-Laying Board

In order to apply the resist paste, you'll need a smooth, flat work surface on which to support your fabric and stencil. The paste-laying board (or *kataita*) serves this purpose. It consists of a sheet of smooth masonite or of very smooth wood, one that is longer and wider than the fabric with which you'll be working. Traditionally, the kataita is covered with a coating of paste which, when moistened, acts as an adhesive to hold the fabric in place. If your board is made of wood, be sure that it isn't rough, varnished, painted, or dirty.

To fasten the fabric to the kataita, Japanese stencil dyers first spread a layer or two of sweet-rice paste,

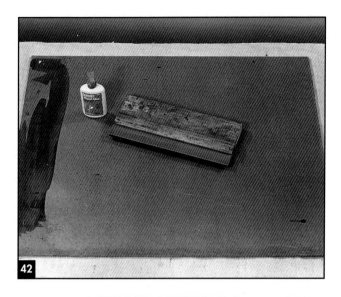

but an easier method for the home dyer is to use either a temporary spray adhesive or a standard white glue instead. To use the spray adhesive, see the next section, "Securing the Fabric."

When using white glue, you'll need a metal spatula or rubber squeegee (Photo 42). Squeeze an ample amount of glue onto your board, and spread it evenly (Photo 43). Allow the glue to dry.

If you would prefer to make a sweet-rice flour (mochiko) paste for the board, first mix together about 1/2 cup (60 g or 118 ml) of sifted sweet-rice flour, three tablespoons (44 ml) of tepid water, and about two teaspoons (13.3 g) of salt. Use your hands to combine these ingredients, adding the water a little at a time. (The salt will prevent the dough from cracking in dry weather; in humid weather, you may not need to add it.)

With your hands, make 1"-diameter (2.54 cm) balls from the dough, and drop them into boiling water. A few minutes after the balls rise to the water's surface, remove them and mash them with a wooden pestle or potato masher, adding a little hot water while you do. The paste should be the consistency of sour cream or wallpaper paste—thin enough to apply with a paint scraper or metal spatula and slightly thinner than the resist paste. Spread this paste evenly on the board. If your board is new, apply at least two coats of paste; wait for the first coat to dry before applying the second.

Securing the Fabric

To secure the fabric to the paste-laying board in the traditional manner and to apply the resist paste through the stencil, you'll need the items shown in Photo 44: resist paste and a wooden spoon; a stiff, flat brush; some sand or sawdust and a small sieve; a pair of cotton clotheslines; several shinshi (bamboo stretchers); a pair of harite (wooden stretchers); a wide, coarse brush; some T-pins; wooden spatulas; and the stencil, fabric, and paste-laying board. You'll also want to have on hand a shallow pan (as large as your stencil), a soft absorbent cloth, and some old newspaper.

About 15 or 20 minutes before you intend to lay the fabric on the board, moisten the glue or paste-covered board with a sprayer or with a coarse brush dipped in water. The pause will give any surface water a chance to settle. If you haven't already done so, trim excess gauze from the stencil's edges. Then submerge the stencil in water for 20 to 30 minutes; soaking the stencil will soften it.

Lift the stencil out of the water (Photo 45), place it on several layers of newspaper, and gently pat it dry with a soft cloth (Photo 46). If you're using temporary spray adhesive instead of white glue or paste, just spray the adhesive onto the bare board at this point. To lay the fabric on the board, position one end at the board's edge; the moistened or sprayed board should be somewhat tacky. Use your palm to press that end of the fabric in place (Photo 47), and then unroll the remaining material onto the board, carefully pressing out all wrinkles and air bubbles (Photo 48). Make sure that the selvage is parallel to the edge of the board. If your piece of fabric is small, position the corners first, and then press the center in place.

After you've attached the fabric to the board, you'll need to place the stencil carefully in position. Make sure that it rests on the fabric with its gauze side up,

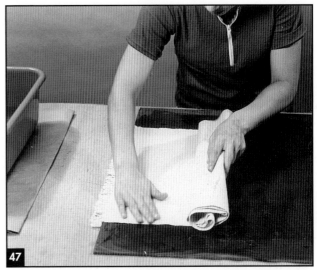

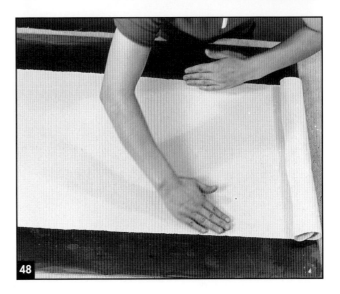

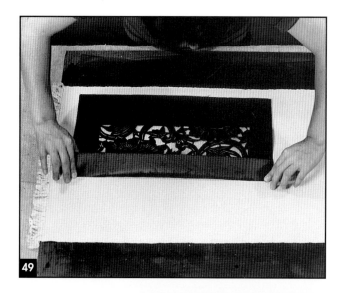

and be sure to leave some fabric free at each end. You'll need to attach these free ends to harite later.

Fold the fuchiba up (Photo 49), and hold it in position by inserting T-pins through the border and into the uncovered fabric behind it (Photo 50) at 6" (15.2 cm) intervals. This raised border will prevent paste from spreading onto the fabric outside the designated design area. After you've repositioned the stencil paper in order to repeat the design, it will also prevent the border from falling into and mashing previously applied paste.

Applying the Resist Paste

The process of applying resist paste is one that is performed with a special spatula known as a hera. Several different sizes and types are available. For general use, select a spatula with a straight, sharp edge about 2-1/2" to 3" (6.4 to 7.6 cm) long. Ideally, this process should be completed during dry weather or in a humidity-controlled environment; the resist paste should dry completely and quickly to be effective. If it's left in humid air for more than three days without drying, the damp paste will mold.

As you work with the spatula, keep two goals in mind: the finished coat of paste should be as thick as the fabric itself, and the paste should penetrate the fabric, not simply sit on its surface. Stand in front of the board, and keep your body at a 45° angle to it, drawing your right foot back. With your spatula, scoop up some resist paste, and begin by placing it at the center of the stencil. The first two strokes of paste, which will stabilize the stencil on the fabric, should run from the center of the stencil upward and from its center downward.

As you make these strokes, hold the spatula lightly, and keep it at a 15° angle to the stencil, regardless of the direction in which the spatula is moving. When you stroke away from yourself, push with your thumb on the spatula's handle; as you stroke towards yourself, press the spatula's handle with your fingers. As you approach the end of a stroke, tilt the spatula to a perpendicular position and flip it quickly, without lifting it up, to start back in the other direction. (In Photo 51, note that the author is working on a repeat.)

Continue to spread paste over the stencil, keeping the blade's edge parallel to the fabric at all times. Two coats of paste should be applied, immediately on top on one another; when you're finished, the carved design will be barely visible (Photo 52). Use your other hand to hold the stencil firmly in place as you stroke, and avoid touching the paste once it's been spread. Keep the bowl of paste on your board, to the right of your work area. If the pattern begins to dry out, its cut edges may curl upward, allowing paste to seep under them. Use a sprayer to mist the pattern with water if you see evidence of this happening.

Each time you remove the spatula, first bring it into a border area. Then tilt it to a perpendicular position, press downward slightly, and pull straight up—all in one fluid motion—so that any extra paste will separate from the pattern.

When you've finished, check carefully to make sure that the paste has gone through every carved area of the stencil. Then carefully remove the stencil, lifting it as if you were turning the page of a large book (Photo 53). Check the paste for air bubbles; remove any that you see by pricking them with a pin.

Before repositioning a stencil for a repeated design, check its back for paste that may have crept from the front. Wipe this excess paste off with a damp cloth. Then hold the upper and lower corners of the left fuchiba and look through the registration marks, carefully matching the marks as you gently drop the stencil in place. If your pattern is a positive design and there's enough space in between the pattern repeats, you may overlap the stencil about 1/8" to 1/4" (.3 to .6 cm).

Once you've re-positioned the stencil, place straight pins through the fuchiba again to keep it perpendicular to the board and away from the paste that has already been applied. Before applying more paste to the stencil, go over its upper surface once with the spatula to force any remaining paste into the fabric.

When you're repeating a pattern both vertically and horizontally, first repeat the pattern in one direction, then in the other. When you get to design areas that lie between previously applied vertical and horizontal sections, first fold the two fuchiba that meet previously stenciled areas. Then fasten them at the corner with a straight pin, and place pins along their lengths to keep them from falling into the paste.

At this point, you'll need to make some decisions based on the thickness of your fabric, its intended use, and your selected method of applying the pigment or dye. If your fabric is fairly thin, and if you'll be applying the pigment or dye with a brush, you

have finished the paste-application process. (If the paste has penetrated the fiber structure properly, your final dyed design will be visible on both surfaces of the fabric.) Remove the stencil and place it in a tray of water, gauze-side down, to soak for 30 minutes to an hour. Then proceed to the steps described in the next section, "Drying the Fabric." After the stencil has soaked thoroughly, remove the paste from it by patting it with a sponge. Treat the stencil as carefully and gently as possible; scrubbing should be avoided as it will damage the stencil and gauze.

If you wish the design to be visible on both surfaces of a thick fabric (perhaps a room-divider), and if you plan to apply dye or pigment with a brush, you may wish to apply paste to both the front and the back of the fabric. Doing so will prevent dye from bleeding

into the paste-covered areas and will ensure crisp, clear design lines. After you've applied paste to the front, leave the fabric on the wooden board until the paste dries; this will prevent shrinkage across the fabric's width and will stop the fabric from curling up at its selvage. Then peel the fabric off the board, turn it over, and place it back on the board, with its pasted surface facing down. Position the stencil on the fabric's back by matching the pattern carefully with the paste that you've already applied on the front; then apply paste to the fabric again. (A light box can be helpful here. By placing the fabric on it, you'll be able to match the paste that you apply to the second side with the paste that you've already applied on the first.)

If you plan to submerse your fabric in indigo, and if you wish to have the design area visible on only one surface of the fabric (as in the case of a wall-hanging), you won't need to apply paste to both fabric surfaces, but you will need to take an extra step. To protect the paste from the effects of submersion, sprinkle sawdust or sand over it while it's still damp (Photo 54). Use a brush to distribute the sand or sawdust evenly (Photo 55). The sand or sawdust will protect the indigo bath from softening (and perhaps dissolving) the paste.

When you plan to submerge your fabric (thick or thin) in either chemical dye or a natural dye other than indigo, you'll need to apply both paste and sawdust or sand to both surfaces of the fabric. Unless you do this, the dye will creep through the fabric's back, under the paste-covered areas on the front, distorting the visible design areas on the fabric's front surface. (Oddly enough, indigo dye, as opposed to other submersion dyes, is less likely to creep in this manner when only one of the fabric's surfaces has been covered with paste and sand, but it's wise to take the precautionary step of applying these substances to both surfaces anyway, especially if your fabric is thick.) And, if you want the design to be visible on both fabric surfaces, as in the case of a room-divider, you'll need to apply paste and sawdust or sand to both surfaces even when you're dyeing with indigo.

Drying the Fabric

After you've applied the paste, removed the pattern, and inspected the paste for air bubbles, you'll need to dry the fabric in full sunlight before you can dye it. Insert each end of the fabric into harite (Photo 56). Make sure that the fabric's edges are clamped straight (Photo 57). Then carefully peel the fabric off the board; pulling it abruptly may cause it to stretch. To remove the fabric evenly, insert a ruler between it and the board; as you peel back the fabric, scrape the ruler toward it. Doing this will keep the fiber structure straight without damaging the paste.

Next, tie rope to both ends of each stretcher; Photos 58-61 illustrate the tying technique. To dry the fabric outdoors, in full sunlight, attach the ropes' ends to two trees or to two poles inserted vertically in the ground, and stretch the fabric, with its paste-covered surface facing up, so that it is flat and level with the ground. If the fabric isn't flat, water may collect in low spots and soften the paste.

Once the fabric has been suspended on harite, fasten shinshi to its back at 4" to 8" (10.2 to 20.3 cm) intervals (Photo 62). The shinshi, which have short brass needles at both ends, are inserted at the very edge of both selvages; they prevent fabric shrinkage and cracking of the resist paste. Keep them level, straight, and parallel to the fabric's woven structure.

57

58

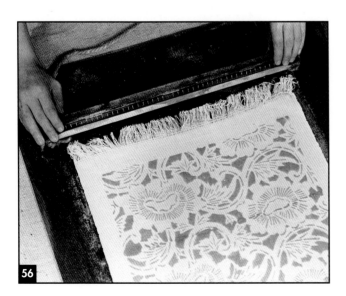

56

59

Keep the fabric stretched after it has dried; a change in weather conditions can cause even dry paste to crack and shrink.

If your design has many intricate, pasted areas, and the paste is on one surface of the fabric only, you may need to take an extra step after attaching the shinshi in order to encourage the paste to penetrate the fiber structure thoroughly. While the paste is still damp, use a large brush to coat the fabric's back with water; then chafe the back surface with a dull knife or metal spatula to draw the paste further into the fiber structure.

CHAPTER SEVEN
SIZING

Before dyeing the fabric, you must apply a *soybean-juice sizing* in order to make the paste durable and to coat the fabric so that dye won't creep under the paste to the fabric's back. The sizing also helps to bind dye and pigment to the fiber. Photo 63 shows the items you'll need to gather in preparation for this step: powdered slaked lime (calcium hydroxide) and a measuring spoon; a cotton bag, double-stitched on three sides, and a large bowl (you'll need two); an electric blender; soaked soybeans; and a 3" to 3-1/2" (7.6 to 8.9 cm) brush.

Making Soybean-Juice Sizing

Keep in mind that liquid sizing will spoil and solidify in high temperatures, so make only as much as you can use at one time, and once you've made it, don't place it in direct sunlight or anywhere near a heat source. Once the powdered slaked lime has been added, the sizing will last one or two months if refrigerated.

To make about one cup (236.6 ml) of liquid sizing, first soak dried soybeans in cold water (overnight during warm weather and for 24 hours during cold weather). Then place one cup (236.6 ml) of the swollen, soaked beans into a blender, and add an equal amount of cold water. Grind the beans and water at high speed for about 15 minutes, until they're the consistency of a milk shake (Photo 64). In Japan, professional artists use an earthenware mortar (or *suribachi*) for this purpose.

65

66

67

Next, add a small amount (about one teaspoon or 3.3 g) of slaked lime to the blender's contents (Photo 65). Then add more water (Photo 66), and blend at low speed for five minutes. Place the cotton bag into an empty bowl, and pour the blended bean mixture into the bag (Photo 67). Squeeze the bag to strain the juice into the bowl (Photo 68), making sure that none of the mixture escapes through the bag's top.

Add some water to a second bowl. Submerge and squeeze the bag in that bowl to collect a second juice (Photo 69); it will be rather thin. In Japanese, these two juices are called *ichiban-go,* (the first juice) and *niban-go,* (the second juice). Mix the two different liquids in the following proportions: two-thirds of the first juice to one-third of the second juice.

Applying the Sizing

You'll apply the sizing to the suspended fabric with a short, wide, absorbent brush called a *naoshi-bake.* Dip the brush into the sizing (Photo 70), squeeze out the excess juice by pressing the brush against the bowl's edge, and lift the brush quickly. Work with 5" to 6" (12.7 to 15.2 cm) fabric sections, brushing back

68

and forth from the left edge of the fabric. Hold the brush lightly with your right hand, placing your thumb on one side of the brush's handle and your four fingers on the opposite side.

As you apply the juice, support the brush instead of pushing it; keep your wrist flexible and your elbow in. Hold the fabric steady with your left hand (Photo 71). Make sure that all areas are evenly covered and that the sizing is absorbed by the fiber structure as much as possible. Sizing that is left to pool on the fabric's surface for too long will soften the paste and damage the design; be sure to spread the juice quickly and well.

Avoid rubbing the surface of the fabric too hard, or you'll loosen the paste in the more delicate design areas. If the fabric is thick, apply juice to its back as well. Turn the fabric over, without removing the shinshi, and brush sizing onto its back (Photo 72), working from left to right again. Make sure that all fabric areas, including the ends, are sized.

As you apply the sizing, re-stretch the fabric by pulling the ropes attached to the stretchers at the fabric's ends (Photo 73), or the weight of the juice will cause the fabric to stretch unevenly. Work in a sunny, dry space, and avoid working on rainy days or late in the evening; unless the fabric dries quickly, the juice won't be effective. Sizing that dries slowly may

70

71

69

72

allow dye to penetrate the paste-covered areas, thus defeating the sizing's original purpose.

While you are waiting for the fabric to dry, prepare your dye or pigment. And don't forget to wash out your brush as soon as you're finished with it, or the sizing will harden the brush and ruin it.

Stencil-dyed rice paper, for making a Japanese fan. Designed by Keisuke Serizawa and executed by unknown artisans.

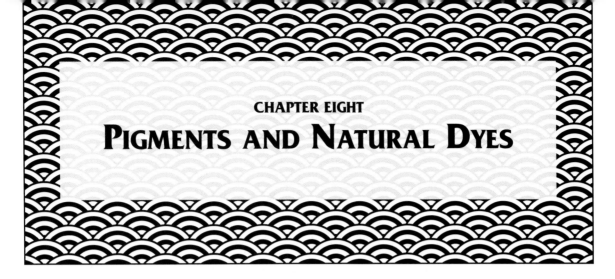

CHAPTER EIGHT
PIGMENTS AND NATURAL DYES

This chapter contains a brief discussion of natural dyes and pigments. With its help you will select and prepare a coloring matter for the next step of kata-zome. (Because so many books are available on dyes, only the bare essentials are covered here.) Instructions for the actual brush-dyeing process are provided in the next chapter.

Dyes, both natural and synthetic, are substances that synthesize with fiber by reacting chemically with it. Some dyes will bond chemically without the addition of *mordants*—substances which serve as bridges between dye molecules and chemical groupings in the fiber molecules. Most natural dyes, however, require the use of mordants to develop their colors.

Unlike dyes, pigments do not react chemically with the fabric or paper to which they're applied; they simply remain on the surface and are bonded to it instead. To dye with pigments, *binding agents* must therefore be used. Colored soil was probably the first pigment ever used and is certainly one of the most convenient to apply, but its rough texture causes it to wear off. India ink, another pigment and one much finer in texture than soil, stays in place a bit longer, but it still requires a binding agent in order to prevent it from fading or wearing out.

Contemporary symmetrical stencil pattern. With this stencil, the author dyed the obi shown on the next page.

Some dyes and pigments are more appropriate for stencil-dyeing than others. Because the resist paste is water-soluble, it's not usually possible to use dyes that require the use of hot water. Dyes that require submersion in cold or lukewarm water can be used, however, if the paste is first coated with sawdust or sand.

Of the many types of dyes and pigments available to the home dyer, several are suitable for Japanese stencil-dyeing. The focus of this chapter and the next is on natural (organic) dyes and pigments (mineral, animal, and cellulose), the dyestuffs used in traditional katazome. These produce beautiful and reliable results. Synthetic dyes may also be used, among them fiber-reactive dyes, direct dyes, acid dyes, and vat dyes. For instructions on their use, see Chapter Thirteen. Azoic (or naphthol) dyes are also used in traditional katazome, but because they are very hazardous to the health, their use isn't covered in this book. Naphthol dyes are no longer widely available; fiber-reactive dyes have taken their place.

Preparations

If you're a complete beginner to dyeing, be sure to familiarize yourself with the standard recipes and safety precautions for the use of natural dyes. Dyeing with natural substances is not especially dangerous, but a few precautions should be taken: don't use cooking utensils or work near food, wear a mask when mixing dry dyes or pigments, wear rubber gloves, make sure your work area is well-ventilated, and don't mix mordant solutions unless you've researched them thoroughly and know what you're doing.

Following are a few tips for care and maintenance of your katazome brushes and other dyeing equipment.

Keep brushes separate. Use different ones for soybean-juice application, for each dye and pigment, and for each mordant; don't interchange them. Label your brushes so that you'll remember which one belongs to each substance.

Always rinse out your brushes as soon as you've finished using them. Don't let soybean juice, dyes, or mordants dry on them.

To rinse a brush, stand it vertically in the palm of your hand, and run cold water over the bristles, gently pressing them down into your palm to squeeze out the residual dye.

To dry your brush, shake the water out of the bristles, and hang the brush vertically on a wall or in the open air.

Clean all other tools, including all containers, before mordants, natural dyes, or chemical dyes have a chance to dry on their surfaces.

Always use non-reactive containers: enamel, glass, or plastic. Never use tin or aluminum containers; these will be damaged by acids, mordants, and other chemical substances.

Opposite page: Symmetrical Composition. *Stencil-dyed obi (Japanese belt) created with the stencil shown on the previous page. The author executed the fusenori technique (explained on pages 58 and 59) with indigo and red (shu) pigment.*

Left and below: *Another stencil-dyed Japanese obi, designed by the author. Fusenori technique with indigo blue.*

Pigments

The pigments listed are all suitable for katazome.

Vermillion (orange, red)

Rouge

Cochineal

Red Oxide

Ochre

Indigo (powdered)

Ultramarine Blue

India ink (Sumi ink)

Gofun

Vellence

Bero (transparent)

Pigments are mixed with a binding agent that facilitates fixing their colors on the fabric or paper to which they're applied. There are several types of binding agents. In Japan, the most popular of these are soybean juice and milk, largely because their proteins prevent them from being water-soluble and hence prevent colors from wearing away when the fabric is washed. Both soybean juice and milk solidify once they are dry, but soybean juice is less water-soluble and has been used for centuries as a binding agent in katazome.

Photo 74 illustrates the necessary equipment for pigment preparation: a mortar and pestle; powdered pigments; a small dish for each pigment that you intend to mix; a measuring spoon; some of the first soybean-juice extraction (ichiban-go); and a palette knife.

First, measure an appropriate amount of pigment into a mortar (Photo 75). Grind the pigment with a pestle until it is very fine-grained and shiny. Then gradually add just enough ichiban-go to dissolve the pigment, mixing as you do. Don't add the pigment to the juice, or it won't dissolve properly. Continue to thin the pigment until you've achieved the desired shade and value (Photo 76), but take care not to make the solution thinner than the sizing that you used earlier. Be sure to mix enough pigment to complete an entire batch of dyeing; batches made midprocess are likely to differ in shade and value.

Some pigments (vermillion and red oxide, for example) are more oily or fine-grained than others. In order to dissolve these, they should be pasted first with a few drops of alcohol.

In recent years, a number of excellent fabric paints have been developed. Feel free to use them instead of the pigments described in this section. As a binding agent with these paints, mix one part ichiban-go (the first soybean-juice extraction; see Chapter Seven) with three parts paint.

Natural Dyes

Natural dyes are most frequently used for background coloring. Those listed in Chart I (see page 97) are suitable for katazome. Select dyes appropriate for your fiber; if you're a beginner, choose just a couple of dyes (I would recommend logwood and catechu), and work with them exclusively.

After you've applied natural dyes, you'll need to develop and fix their colors with mordants. Appropriate mordants and the color ranges they create are indicated in Chart I (on page 97). Other mordants exist for use with natural dyes; copper sulfate (cupric sulfate) and ferrous sulfate (ferric sulfate) are among them. Lime is not recommended as a mordant; it fixes colors rather weakly.

To make a mordant solution, first dissolve 1-1/3 oz. (37.8 g) of mordant in a little water. Add cold water to make up one cup (236 ml) of solution. Following are dilution proportions for each mordant.

- Alum: Thin three to five times
- Potassium bichromate: Thin ten times
- Ferrous sulfate: Thin thirty times
- Copper sulfate: Thin between five and eight times

The effects of mordants on color development are greatly (and differently) affected by the weather. Potassium bichromate, for example, requires direct sunlight, or color development will be insufficient. Ferrous sulfate, on the other hand, must be applied in the shade and then moved into direct sunlight; it develops its color so rapidly that you'll see color changes before you've finished applying it.

Each of these solutions should be applied after the second coat of dye has dried. Use either a 2″ to 3″ (5.1 to 7.6 cm) brush or, if you are fixing irosashi

colors (see Chapter Nine), with a small brush. Remember to wash your brush thoroughly as soon as you've used it with any given mordant or, better yet, use a different brush for each mordant. Combinations of mordants on your brush will cause disastrous results. And don't let the brush dry out before you clean it.

Soon after any of these solutions is applied with a brush, the dye will turn a bright and rich color. To obtain even results on both the front and back of the fabric, don't turn the fabric over before it has dried. After the mordant dries, apply another coat of dye solution, but dilute this dye until it is three times thinner than the last coat you applied.

Indigo

Indigo dye must undergo a complex fermentation process similar to that used in making wine. In Japan, because there has been such a high demand for indigo-dyed fabrics, this is done by specialists, who make their decoctions in vats approximately ten feet deep and five feet wide. These vats are set in the ground, where correct temperatures for fermenting the decoctions and for establishing correct consistencies and colors can be maintained. A dyer usually has at least ten vats of indigo, varying in shades from light to dark. When customers bring their pasted fabrics, they specify the shade they'd like, and the dyer soaks the fabric in the appropriate vat.

Chapter Nine provides instructions for applying vatted indigo, but stencil dyers who wish to vat their own dye will need to find recipes elsewhere.

Fixers

Fixers reinforce color fastness; they're brushed onto the fabric after pigments (or pigments and dyes) have been applied. When both dye and pigment have been used on the same piece of fabric, a *formalin* solution should be used as a fixer. To prepare this solution, mix one teaspoonful (5 ml) of formalin with one gallon (3.8 liters) of cold water. After the fabric has dried, apply this solution with a brush. When only pigments have been used on the fabric, use *alum* instead of formalin. Prepare the alum solution by mixing one tablespoon (15 ml) of alum with one gallon (3.8 liters) of cold water.

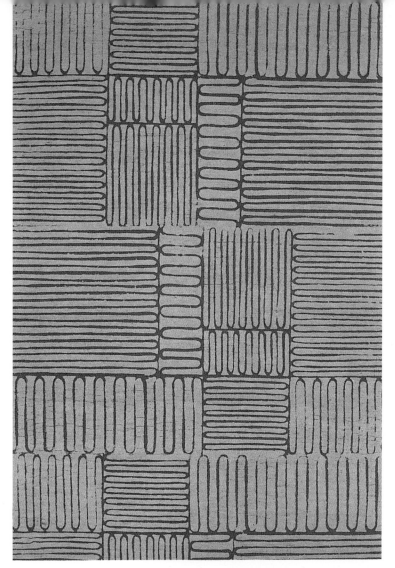

Left: Geometrical Composition. *Stencil-dyed Japanese obi (or belt).*

Below: *Detail of another stencil-dyed obi.*

Opposite page: *This long-sleeved kimono is typical of those traditionally worn by women on their twentieth birthday and then only on special occasions until they are married. Design by Keisuke Serizawa; execution, with indigo blue and pigment, by Kiyoto Shimodaira.*

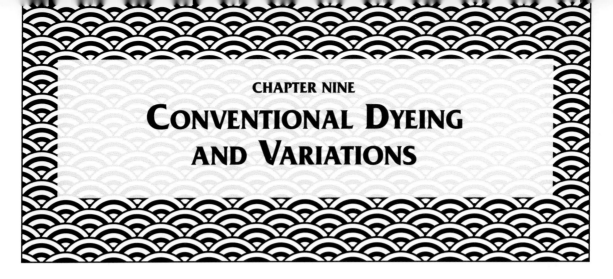

CHAPTER NINE
CONVENTIONAL DYEING AND VARIATIONS

After the soybean-juice sizing has dried, your fabric will be ready for dyeing. There are several different sequences in which you may execute katazome; a list of these is given in Chapter Two. This chapter covers the conventional, three-stage katazome technique as well as a number of variations. In Chapter Ten, the freehand paste-resist method known as tsutsugaki-zome is described, and Chapter Eleven offers explanations of alternative paste-resist methods.

Conventional Method

In the conventional method, small portions of the area not protected by paste are colored first. Then these detail areas must be covered with resist paste so that the remaining portions of the design area can be dyed with a background (or base) color, often a dark one. The paste is applied with a *tsutsu* (or conical tube); refer to Chapters Two and Ten for further information. Traditional bingata patterns are dyed in this fashion.

Stage One: Irosashi

The process of dyeing detail areas (select portions of the design areas that are not covered by paste) is known as irosashi. Colors may be placed as you wish—through careful planning, with color schemes conceived as you design your pattern, or through spontaneous decision-making as you apply the pigments. Of course, you'll need to have a rough idea of any repeats and their sequence before you start.

To minimize the effects of the wind, irosashi is usually completed indoors, but the dye or pigment must dry quickly. Slow drying may cause the paste to soften, especially at the edges of paste-defined areas, and the result will be indistinct edges between dyed and undyed areas. Whether you complete this step indoors or out, the fabric should remain on harite, and the shinshi should be left in place.

Pour the top portion of the dissolved pigment into a container, and use a small brush to fill in the detail areas. You may test the color by applying a bit to a

Shown on page 58 is a piece of rice paper dyed with this contemporary stencil pattern.

border area at one end of the fabric or to a swatch of the same fabric. Hold the brush perpendicular to the surface of the fabric (Photo 77); if you use the brush's side, the pigment will not penetrate the fiber structure thoroughly.

Apply the pigment by moving the brush in small circles, working gradually from the outside of the area to be colored toward the inside. Don't worry about overlapping color onto the paste, but avoid working pigment excessively at the paste's edges. Take care not to let the section you're working on dry out as you re-moisten your brush, or the color in that area will appear uneven. If you intend to use more than one color, complete the filling-in process with the first color, and then proceed to the next color (Photo 78). Use one brush for each different color so that the colors won't get muddy.

Avoid trying to brighten colors by piling them up in thick layers. Instead, apply a first coat of each color, letting each one dry thoroughly, and then apply another, thinner coat, one color at a time. Make sure that the colors don't remain in one spot like stains; try to spread them evenly.

Irosashi colors may be emphasized by applying gradation coloring; adding shading to partially colored design parts (the tips of leaves, the borders between two different colors, or large areas that need variations to render them more delicate and interesting) is an important aspect of irosashi. Pigments are applied on top of irosashi colors with a small brush; they're then quickly feathered out with a dry brush. By blending shades gradually, a three-dimensional effect is created.

The standard colors used for gradation are red, blue, purple, and black in various shades. Most bingata-zome patterns include gradations; you can easily create your own method of gradation by selecting colors and placing them in a manner that is consistent with your design. Of course, you may eliminate gradation if you feel it is proper to do so for the design you are executing.

Once you've finished irosashi, you'll need to apply a fixer to maintain the color fastness of the pigment. You may use alum, or you may dissolve formalin in water, in a 1:300 ratio. Then use a small brush to apply either the top part of the alum solution or the formalin to each small, dyed section of the pattern. When the fabric has dried completely, proceed to fusenori—protecting these dyed areas with paste so that the background can be dyed (Photo 79).

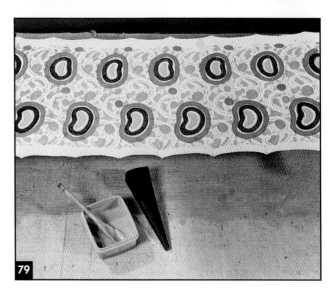

Stage Two: Fusenori

Fusenori is a technique that protects previously dyed areas from subsequent coats of pigment. Irosashi areas are covered with resist paste to prevent the background (or base) color from entering them.

To make the resist paste used in fusenori, follow the directions for making katazome resist paste on pages 33–37, but make this paste slightly more sticky by adding about one-tenth more sweet-rice flour. This paste is applied with the conical tube used in

tsutsugaki-zome; for a full description of this tube, see page 69.

Once you've prepared the paste, fill about two-thirds of the tube by scooping paste into it (Photo 80). Next, cover the irosashi areas by squeezing resist paste out of the tube (Photo 81). Use your fingertip to spread the paste evenly (Photo 82). Try to keep the resist paste off the background areas that you plan to dye, but don't worry excessively about being accurate. The results of an occasional error in paste application can

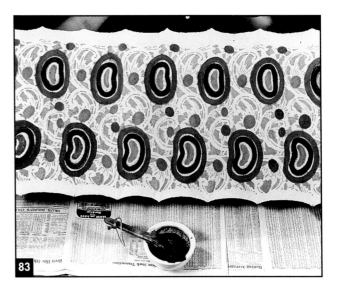

actually result in a rather interesting and enjoyable finished appearance.

Note, too, that if you'd like to create outlines around irosashi areas, outlines that will be the color of your original fabric, or if you'd like to modify your stencil-applied design by protecting additional, original fabric areas from your chosen, dyed background colors, you may use the fusenori paste to do so. Allow the paste to dry thoroughly, in mild sunlight (Photo 83).

Stage Three: Dyeing the Background

Once all irosashi areas are protected by paste, you may dye the remaining design area with a selected base color. Perform this step outdoors, in full sunlight, as the pigment must dry quickly. If you're working in partial shade, shift the fabric as it dries to ensure that each portion receives its share of sunlight.

Opposite page: This rice paper was dyed using the stencil pictured on page 56 and the tsutsugaki technique described in Chapter Ten.

Right: *Another contemporary design of the author's, also executed on rice paper using the tsutsugaki method.*

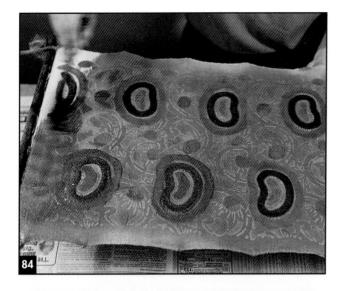

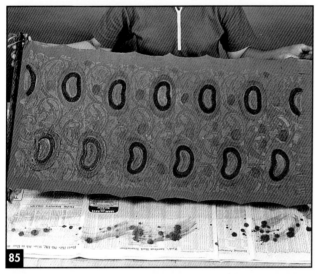

Apply the pigment much as you applied the soybean-juice sizing. Place the top portion of the pigment solution (some of the pigment will have settled) into a pail or bucket, and stir it thoroughly. Dip a wide brush—the same size as the one with which you brushed on the sizing—into the pigment, and then squeeze out the extra solution by pressing the brush against the pail's top edge.

Brush the solution onto the entire fabric, working from left to right and aiming for even results without lines, streaks, or different shades of color (Photo 84). To obtain even distribution of the pigment, stir the solution thoroughly each time you dip the brush into it. Picking up an equal amount of solution on the brush each time you dip it will help you to obtain even colors.

After each application, shake all excess pigment from your brush, and go over the surface of the fabric with this relatively dry brush to encourage even penetration of the pigment. (Don't attempt this with fine-lined design patterns; you may rub the paste off the fabric.) Avoid pressing, bending, or twisting the brush, and don't rub it into the fabric. Instead, hold the brush gently, perpendicular to the fabric's surface. Extend your brush strokes as far as possible in each direction. When you are working on a long piece of fabric, you can avoid streaking as you move down the fabric's length by overlapping the strokes that you made in one position with those made in the next position by 2" to 3" (5.1 to 7.6 cm).

Generally speaking, colors will look much brighter when the fabric is wet. To judge whether or not the shade of the dried color will be bright enough, hold the fabric up to light and look through its back. What you see will be the approximate shade of the dried color.

For the richest and brightest possible colors, apply two thin coats of the pigment solution, rather than a single, concentrated coat. The second coat should be slightly thinner than the first and should be applied after the first has dried. Photos 85 and 86 show the front and back of the dyed fabric.

To store leftover pigment solution for later use, cover it with water; the pigment will settle at the bottom of the container. Pour the water off when you're ready to use the solution.

Don't turn the fabric over before it dries out, or the shinshi may touch the fabric's back, leaving unsightly marks. When you wish to dye both sides of the fabric, quickly move the shinshi to the fabric's front. Then dye the back of the fabric, wait until the first coat dries, and repeat to apply a second coat. After the fabric has dried, you'll need to apply a fixer once again.

After the formalin or alum has dried, leave the fabric in the open air for at least one to two days (or even up to one week), so that the dye or pigment will settle into the fiber structure thoroughly, and the color will look richer and deeper. Then take out the shinshi and remove the fabric from the harite. Carefully fold the fabric in large sections so that the paste isn't damaged.

Variation A: Dyeing the Background First
In this time-saving variation, the conventional method is reversed and fusenori is omitted. Once the sizing has dried, the background color is applied, outdoors, to the entire paste-covered fabric with a wide brush. When the fabric has dried thoroughly, detail colors are applied on top of the background color. The background color must be fairly light, and the detail colors that will be placed on top of it must blend with it in an attractive manner. Avoid color combinations that are muddy or especially dark.

Variation B: Sashi-Wake
Sashi-wake, a method that provides delicate and elegant results, is the process of using several colors to fill in all the design areas not protected by paste. Pigments are applied to the fabric, one at a time, much as they are in irosashi, but all paste-free sections are filled in—

no base color is applied afterward. The small brushes used in this method are called *sashi-bake* or *so-sashi*.

Variation C: Atosashi
A third variation permits you to refine previously applied opaque pigments by adding transparent pigments on top of them; this process is known as atosashi (or final touch). Atosashi differs from gradation in that it refines existing colors rather than shading them. In terms of effect, irosashi (coloring small areas on an undyed background) and atosashi (coloring areas already dyed) are also quite different.

Atosashi requires careful selection of colors; it can be difficult to establish complementary relationships between background and detail colors when one is applied on top of another, but when colors are selected correctly, the results are truly beautiful.

It is also possible to combine the use of dyes and pigments in this method, but if you choose to experiment in this manner, be sure to apply transparent dyes on top of opaque pigments.

Variation D: Dyeing a Single Color
In order to practice pigment or dye application, beginners may want to dye their entire design a single color. To do this, simply follow the instructions for applying a background coat.

Indigo (Aizome)
Indigo, which yields colors so clear and beautiful that professional dyers in Japan often use it exclusively,

Traditional, realistic, bingata stencil pattern.

Above: *Both pieces of rice paper were dyed with the same traditional bingata stencil pattern, but the author has varied the color schemes. Note the gradation coloring in the upper piece.*

Opposite page: *Contemporary design on rice paper, executed using the tsutsugaki method (see Chapter Ten).*

requires special treatment to prepare. This dye is not water-soluble; it must be reduced so that it can be dissolved in an alkali solution. Vat recipes are available in books on indigo dyeing.

Once you have prepared the vat, you will need to dip your fabric in it, rather than apply the dye with a brush. For the richest possible color, the fabric should be dipped two to five times depending upon the shade you wish to achieve. (Don't forget that when you dye with indigo, you'll need to protect the resist paste by covering it with sand or sawdust before dipping the fabric.) The fabric is then removed from the vat and left in the open air. There the indigo combines with oxygen and changes from greenish-yellow to its final, deep, clear blue.

To combine natural dyes and indigo, first soak the fabric in the indigo-blue vat, and dry the fabric in the open air. Then dye with hematin or logwood by repeating this process several times over the indigo blue background. Finally, use ferrous sulfate (ferric sulfate) as a mordant to set the color. The result will be a rich, deep black. There are many different ways to use various combinations for unusual colors. Experiment, by all means!

Steaming

Ideally, fabrics dyed with pigments, natural dyes, direct dyes, and fiber-reactive dyes should be steamed in order to make the colors fast, to encourage bright and rich colors, and to set the colors into the fiber structure completely. (An alternate treatment for heat-setting fiber-reactive dyes on pasted fabrics is provided in Chapter Thirteen.)

If your fabric is under two yards in length, just use an ordinary enamel canner. For medium-sized pieces of fabric, two to five yards (91.4 to 274.2 cm) in length, commercial steamers are available, but it's fairly easy to make a steamer yourself. First, cut the bottom out of a large garbage can. Then punch two small holes in the very top part of the can's edge, one on each side, level and across from one another. Push a 1/4"-diameter (.6 cm) metal rod (available at hardware stores) through the holes to create a support from which to hang the fabric (see Illustration A on the next page). If you're using an enamel canner, just place a piece of flat, wooden molding across the canner's top. A similar steamer can be made by shaping a large sheet of galvanized tin into a chimney shape and soldering its long edges together.

To prepare the fabric, lay it on a sheet of old newspaper that is slightly larger than the fabric itself. Lay another sheet of newspaper on top. Fold the fabric lengthwise in accordion pleats, and then fold it the same way across its width. This will permit the steam to penetrate all areas of the fabric equally. Tie the folded fabric and paper with strings or cords, just as you would tie a package, crossing the cord over the folded fabric and leaving a looped length to suspend from the rod or molding in the steamer.

To steam your fabric, fill the bottom of a large pan (or the canner if you're using one) with 3" to 4" (7.6 to 10.2 cm) of water. To generate an even flow of steam from the water-filled pan through the fabric (which will hang in the steamer's center), place the pan under the steamer, chimney, or canner so that steam will rise through the steamer's center. Make sure that the pan isn't too large, or steam will escape rather than funneling through the steamer's inside.

Before hanging the fabric in place, bring the water to a boil. Then position the wrapped fabric by hanging it

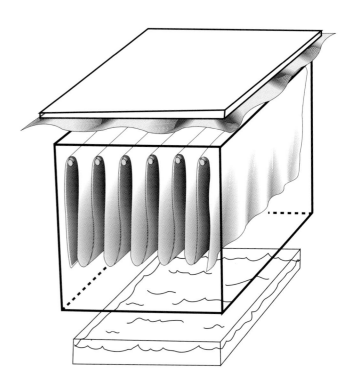

Illustration B

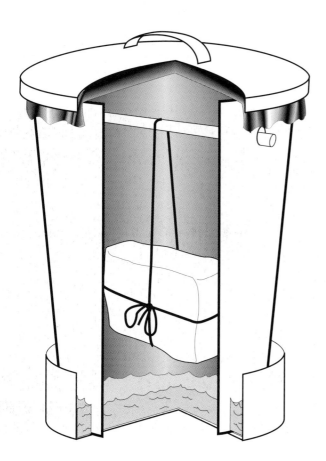

Illustration A

vertically on the metal rod or wooden molding. The folded fabric should hang straight up-and-down in the steamer's center and must not touch the steamer's top, bottom, or sides. Steam that condenses on the steamer's surfaces will cause stains on any fabric section that touches those surfaces, so position your fabric carefully.

Cover the steamer's open top with an old, clean towel or rag. This layer will absorb condensed water and will prevent it from dripping onto the fabric. If you're using one of the homemade steamers, place a thick wooden board (or the garbage-can lid) on top of the towel or rag. A yard (91.4 cm) of medium-thick fabric should be steamed for 30 to 40 minutes.

Very long pieces of fabric, five to ten yards (274.2 to 914 cm) in length will require an even larger steamer. Construct a rectangular wooden frame (see Illustration B), 60" (152.4 cm) wide by 60" (152.4 cm) high by 70" (177.8 cm) long. The frame's 70" length will allow you to steam fabric that is up to 60" in width.

Next, drill holes, 10" (25.4 cm) apart along each top edge of the frame's 60"-wide (152.4 cm) ends, about 3" to 4" (7.6 to 10.2 cm) from the top of the frame.

Make these holes just large enough to accommodate lengths of plastic (PVC) piping. Insert the pipes so that they run lengthwise across the top portion of the wooden frame.

Next, make or purchase a stainless steel water-pan that will fit just inside the bottom of the wooden frame and that is deep enough to hold 4" to 5" (10.2 to 12.7 cm) of boiling water. A close fit will prevent steam from escaping when the water in the pan is brought to a boil.

Drape your fabric over the pipes, as shown in the illustration. Make sure that the fabric portions that rest on the pipes lie well below the top of the frame, and that the lowest portions are at least 5" to 6" (12.7 to 15.2 cm) above the water. The fabric should not touch any portion of the frame or its lid and must not be spattered by boiling water. Cover the frame with absorbent material (toweling, for example) and a large board so that steam won't escape from the top of the frame. Steam the fabric for approximately 45 minutes.

Mizumoto (Removing the Resist Paste)

After steaming, the fabric will first need to be cooled and then the resist paste must be washed from it. You'll need a large sink or an enamel, plastic, or stainless steel tub. Ideally, the tub should be as broad as the fabric is wide and deep enough to hold the fabric without letting it touch the sides. If possible, keep two identical tubs so that you can wash the fabric in the first tub and then move it into a second tub for a thorough rinse.

Fill the first tub with water, and then fold the fabric in accordion layers. Place the folded fabric into the water, holding it carefully by one corner so that the resist paste won't crack. Especially thin fabric may rip, so treat it very carefully. Once the entire fabric has been soaked, draw it toward you, and then push it back into the water to remove all air bubbles. Leave the submerged fabric in the water for at least one hour (Photo 87). The resist paste will soften and loosen automatically and will rise to the fabric's surface.

If the dye is too muddy or the mordant hasn't been sufficiently developed, excess dye may bleed into the water, a process known in Japan as *naku* (or crying). If this should happen, move the fabric as quickly as

possible into another clear tub full of cold water, or the dye will re-enter the fabric, creeping under the areas covered with resist paste.

As soon as the paste has loosened, pull the selvage of the fabric both diagonally and horizontally (Photo 88). Most of the paste should come off as you stretch the fabric in this fashion. To remove even more paste, use a soft, 2" to 3" (5.1 to 7.6 cm) utility brush to gently rub the surface of the fabric where paste is visible

89

90

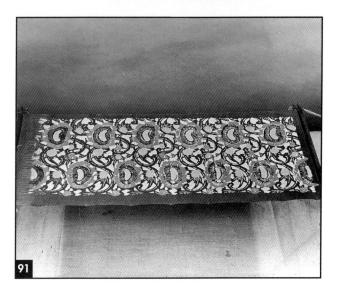

91

(Photo 89). Excessive rubbing may cause pigments to come off, so do be careful. Change the water at least twice during the washing process, and examine the fabric thoroughly for residual paste (Photo 90).

Sometimes the resist paste won't come off as quickly as it should. There are several possible causes: you may have used too much paste; humid air can prevent the calcium hydroxide (slaked lime) in the resist paste from being effective; the lime may have become acidic; and if the paste freezes at all during cold weather, it may be rendered ineffective. All these phenomena are called *kuinori* (sick paste). If the paste is stubborn, leave the fabric in hot water for at least five hours, and then pat it gently with your hands instead of rubbing it. Patience will reward you!

After the visible paste has been removed, leave the fabric submerged for at least one hour to remove any remaining traces. Then use a small brush to rub any residual paste from the surface of the fabric. Lift the fabric out of the water, and drain the water from it by hanging it on a clothesline. Then spin it in a washing machine (on the gentle cycle), and stretch it outdoors on harite once again (Photo 91). To keep the colors from fading in sunlight, make sure to suspend the fabric with its reverse side facing up. Attach shinshi on the dyed side, at 12" (30.48 cm) intervals, to keep the selvage straight while the fabric dries. Remove them after the fabric has dried completely.

It is possible to add to or correct the design after mizumoto. Doing so, however, requires a high level of expertise and is not recommended for beginners.

Opposite page, top: *A typical komon design (characterized by small, scattered design elements) executed on rice paper.*

Opposite page, bottom: *Contemporary design executed on rice paper.*

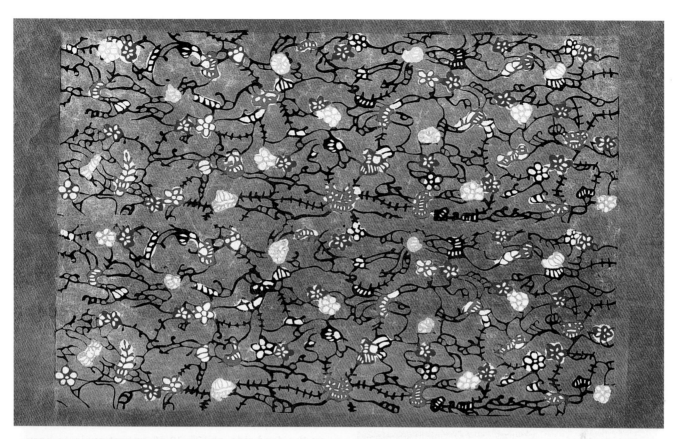

CHAPTER TEN
TSUTSUGAKI-ZOME

Tsutsugaki-zome (also known as *tsutsugaki, noribiki, norigaki,* and *tenori*) is a brother to both katazome and batik. This technique makes use of resist paste just as katazome does and is similar to batik in that the resist is applied directly to the fabric rather than through a stencil. The paste is applied freehand by squeezing it out through the tip of a conical tube (or tsutsu), much as one would decorate a cake with icing. In Japan, several styles of tsutsugaki-zome exist, including *chaya-zome* (a style used for everyday clothing) and *yuzen-zome* (characteristic of designs created for the aristocracy).

Tsutsugaki is conceptually different from katazome in that its expression is much more spontaneous; there are no particular design restrictions such as those imposed by repeating stencil patterns. When you use a stencil to execute an arabesque design on a white background, for example, the continuity of pattern lines and the limits of the design as a whole are always a concern. But when you create a similar design using tsutsugaki, you merely draw the design with the tube rather than having to match registration marks.

Traditionally, tsutsugaki tends to have larger background areas than katazome, a softer, freer, and less complex design, and is often dyed with a single color. One exception is the *sekidashi* method, in which many colors are used.

Photo 92 shows the items you'll need for tsutsugaki: fabric, two pieces of rope, resist paste, a container, a wooden spoon, sand or sawdust, a pair of harite, several shinshi, a flat brush, a narrow spatula, the tsutsu, metal tips for the tsutsu, and a charcoal pencil.

Stage One: Drawing the Pattern

Though they're drawn freehand, tsutsugaki designs are still conceptually similar to stencil designs; hinata (negative), kage (positive), and kukuri (outlined) design concepts all apply. But whether they're found in Okinawan scarves or mainland Japanese kimonos, tsutsugaki designs are quite distinct from those created with other paste-resist techniques.

Drawing the pattern (a process known as *shita-e*) can be done in two ways. In the first method, the pattern is drawn to actual size on a sheet of paper, using a felt-tipped pen or a brush and India ink. The paper is then placed on a light table, so that back-lighting makes the lines clearly visible. Next, the fabric is placed on top of the drawing, and the lines are traced onto the fabric with a charcoal pencil or fabric marker. The second method calls for drawing the pattern directly onto the fabric (Photo 93).

After you've drawn the pattern, stretch the fabric on harite, and attach shinshi to the fabric's back at 4"

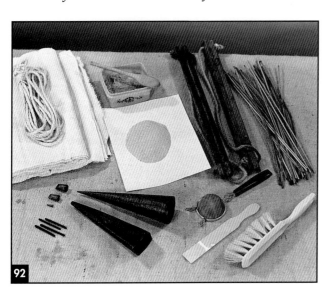

92

to 8" (10.2 to 20.3 cm) intervals. Depending on the width of the fabric, you may substitute a canvas stretcher instead, using thumb tacks to keep the fabric in place, or you may build a wooden frame of the correct size. The goal is to keep the fabric flat and straight.

Stage Two: Making the Resist Paste and Preparing the Tube

To make a resist paste that is slightly stickier than that used in katazome, mix the flour and bran in a ratio of 1:1 or six parts of sweet-rice flour to four parts of rice bran. Increasing the proportion of flour lends more stickiness to the paste. (Note that the flour and bran in the resist paste play similar roles to the beeswax and paraffin in batik resists. The flour imparts stickiness; beeswax prevents cracking. The bran controls the paste's stickiness; paraffin provides a crackled effect.)

The conical tube used in tsutsugaki is made from the same persimmon paper used to make the stencils for katazome, but because it is heavier and stronger, it can withstand squeezing. Tubes in several sizes and thicknesses are available, so select a size that is most compatible with the kind of design and type of lines you intend to draw. (You may improvise a cone from flexible vinyl if you wish.) Removable brass tips can be ordered as well; these attach to the cone's tip and will enable you to vary the size of your design lines. Choose tips, which come in round and flat shapes, both large and small, to suit your design needs.

Before you use the tsutsu, soak it in water for 20 to 30 minutes until it becomes pliable. Next, wipe off the water and cut about 3/8" (1 cm) off the tube's tip to create a small hole. Insert the brass tip (Photo 94) by using a narrow spatula to push it down as far as it will go. If you don't plan to use a metal tip, cut off only 1/4" (.6 cm) from the tube's tip.

With a wooden spoon, fill about two-thirds of the tube with resist paste (Photo 95). Hold the tube between your thumb and forefinger, and push the paste down to the bottom by gradually squeezing the air out. Then seal the tube's top by folding it over a couple of times; this will prevent the paste from oozing out as you apply it.

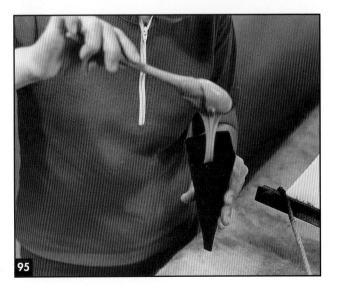

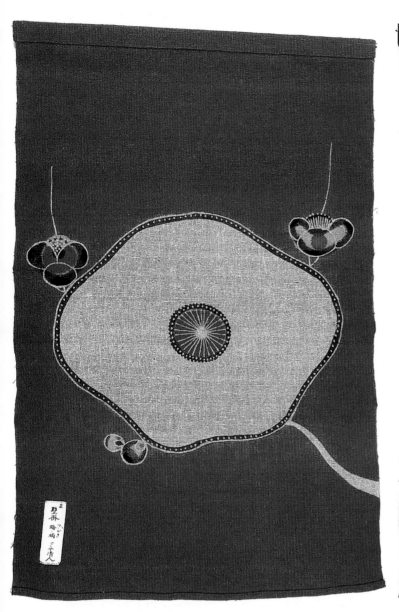

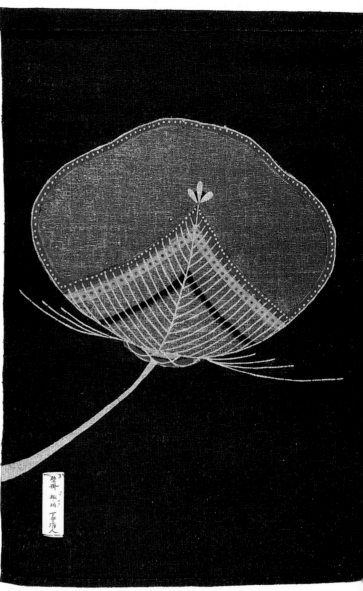

Pine Tree *and* Plum Tree. *Tsutsugaki wall-hangings designed and executed by Kiyoto Shimodaira.*

Stage Three: Applying the Paste

Begin by holding the paste-filled tube perpendicular to and touching the fabric. Squeeze the tube at its top with your thumb and forefinger. As soon as the paste starts coming out, move the tube, holding it at a 60° to 70° angle as you draw over your sketched design (Photo 96). The layer of paste should be thicker than the layer applied in the katazome process. Be sure to press the metal tip into the fabric so that the paste penetrates the fibers properly. Keep the fabric from shifting by holding it with your left hand, and use your right hand to manipulate the tube. Avoid touching previously applied paste; work from one end of the fabric to the other.

When you wish to stop a line, stand the tube straight up again, press down with the tube's tip, and then release all pressure while lifting the tube up off the fabric. Moisten the metal tip with a damp cloth every once in a while to keep its surface smooth and to obtain sharp, clear lines.

If you need to make thicker lines or larger design areas than the ones your metal tips can create, first use a tip to draw the outline of the design area, and then fill in the interior by using either a tube without an attached tip or a fingertip if the area is large enough to do so. If the inside of the design area is wider than the tube's opening, use a narrow spatula to spread the paste instead. And if the area is very wide, use a wide spatula. No matter how the paste is applied, always make sure that it penetrates the fiber structure thoroughly and doesn't just sit on the fabric's surface.

After you've applied paste to the entire design area, use a very narrow spatula or your fingertip to make sure that the paste is spread evenly (Photo 97). As soon as you're finished, sprinkle sand or sawdust over the paste while it's still damp (Photo 98). Before the paste dries out, moisten the bristles of a soft brush, and gently wipe the sand-covered paste's surface with them to eliminate any air bubbles (Photo 99). The paste will be quite soft at this stage, so be careful not to inadvertently alter your design.

100

101

Next, place shinshi at 4" to 6" (10.2 to 15.2 cm) intervals across the fabric's back (Photo 100). If you notice that the paste has failed to go through the fabric, dampen the fabric's back with a sprayer, and then scrape it gently with a dull knife, a palette knife, or an ice scraper. Doing so will draw the paste through the cloth.

Unless you plan to apply paste to the other side of the fabric, you may now dry the fabric in indirect sunlight (Photo 101). Then you'll be ready to work through the remaining steps, following the instructions given in Chapters Seven, Eight, and Nine.

If you plan to apply the paste to both sides, however, be sure to dampen the front of the fabric in order to encourage the paste to penetrate through to the back. As soon as the fabric has dried, move the shinshi from the back to the front so that you can work on the fabric's back surface. Next, repeat the pattern that you applied to the front onto the fabric's back, using the tsutsu and being as accurate as possible; you should be able to see the first design through the material. If the fabric dries too quickly, and the design is no longer visible, dampen it again while you're applying the paste to the back. When you're through, dry the fabric in indirect sunlight.

When you're working with a very large design, one that requires two or more pieces of fabric, you can ensure a well-matched design on the pieces by sewing them together back-to-back and applying resist paste first to one side of the sewn fabric and then to the other.

The remaining processes (applying soybean-juice sizing, brushing on pigment or dye, fusenori, dyeing the background, mizumoto, and so forth), are almost exactly the same as those of katazome. Because the paste used in tsutsugaki is stickier and is applied more thickly than katazome paste, however, mizumoto (rinsing out the resist paste) may take more time. Even when the paste looks soft, it can still be hard underneath. Take your time and be patient! Don't scrub the fabric too hard. Instead, gently rub the fabric's back (never its front) with a spoon or your fingernail.

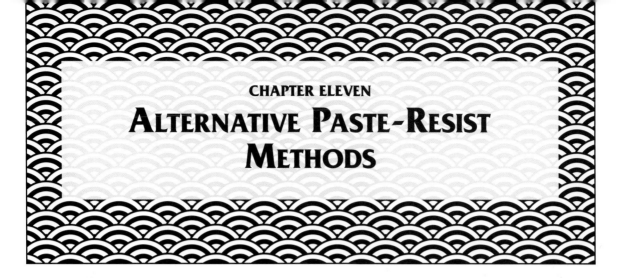

CHAPTER ELEVEN
ALTERNATIVE PASTE-RESIST METHODS

Combining Katazome and Tsutsugaki-Zome

For a more sophisticated look, katazome and tsut-sugaki-zome techniques may be combined. This may be done in either of two ways.

Method One
This first method is one that is used in the traditional bingata style known as *kaeshi-gata*. Katazome is executed first, but rather than leaving the fabric white after mizumoto, the tsutsu tube is used to cover almost all of the colored design areas except for some very fine lines. Then very light shades of pink, yellow, or blue pigment are applied with a brush both to the white background area and to those fine lines within previously colored areas.

Because these light shades not only color the white background fabric but also overlap partially colored areas, a beautiful shadow effect is created,

lending a three-dimensional quality to the finished piece. Additionally, paste applied with the conical tube softens the design features, providing a serendipitous charm that the Japanese value for its very imperfection.

When executing this technique, moisten the back of the fabric after the tsutsu paste has been applied, but avoid scraping the fabric's back with a knife. And use a thinner soybean juice when mixing the background pigment than when mixing the detail-area (irosashi) pigments. (Use niban-go, the second juice extracted for the soybean-juice sizing. See Chapter Seven for instructions.)

Method Two
In Japan, traditional *chugara* (medium-sized) and komon (small-sized) patterns are often used on fabrics that are made for mattresses or coats. Using the katazome stencil, small and medium designs are placed on the fabric. The remaining large areas are

This geometrical stencil pattern was overlapped to dye the haori (or coat) fabric that is pictured on page 75.

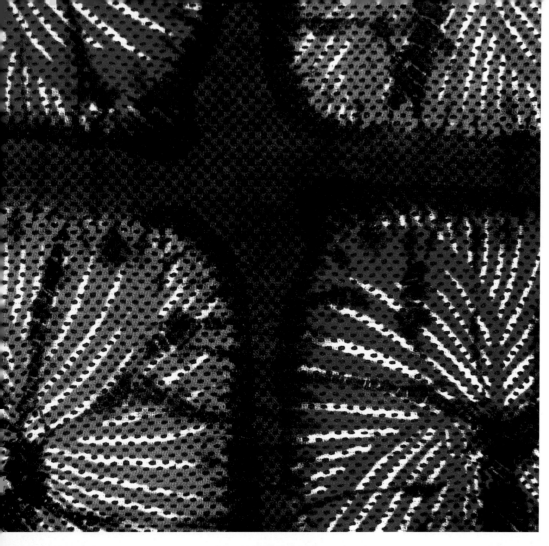

Left: The Sun Early in the Morning *(detail). The author dyed this wall-hanging by combining katazome and shibori.*

Below: Karakusa. *A table runner created by combining katazome and tsutsugaki-zome techniques. The black-and-white photos in Chapter Nine show this piece being created.*

Opposite page: Lines and Lines. *The author dyed this haori (or coat) fabric by over-lapping a single pattern (the kasane technique). The pattern she used is shown on page 73.*

subsequently divided by solid lines and patterns that are created by applying paste with the tsutsu tube. This combination of techniques creates strong contrasts between crisp, structured, and hard-edged composition and soft, spontaneously-drawn tsutsugaki patterns and lines, made in a carefree and non-structured fashion.

To execute this method, first decide exactly where you are going to place the katazome design. Then complete katazome, leaving spaces for the execution of tsutsugaki-zome. After you've applied paste through the stencil, stretch the fabric and fasten shinshi at 6" (15.2 cm) intervals across the fabric's back. Then execute tsutsugaki-zome in the areas not covered by paste. All other steps are exactly the same as those used in the usual tsutsugaki method.

Combining Katazome and Shibori-Zome (Tie-Dyeing)

Though this book does not include an explanation of tie-dyeing (shibori) techniques, these are easily learned; many books on the subject exist. Once you've mastered tie-dyeing, you can combine this

ancient method with katazome to add extra dimensions to your repertoire of stencil-dyeing techniques.

This method can be executed with almost any kind of design. The katazome is completed first. Then the fabric is tied with threads (sometimes reinforced with rubber bands) or dental floss, twisted by hand, or sewn with sewing thread or buttonhole thread, and shibori is completed in order to achieve an intricate design.

Combining Tsutsugaki-Zome and Shibori-Zome

This technique requires that tsutsugaki-zome be completed first and shibori-zome afterward. Be sure to choose a shibori design that will suit your tsutsugaki design; otherwise, there's no reason to go through this rather complicated process.

When it's successful, this combination offers results that are dynamic in ways that no other method can produce. Only the free expression of tsutsugaki combined with the delicate, graceful expression of shibori can create the mysterious and subtle beauty of this dyeing technique.

Don't worry about being neat or about executing a technically perfect design with this method. Instead, relax and express your design naturally. You'll develop creative ideas as you practice, so don't be discouraged if you fail. Overcoming frustration and failure is much like conquering a mountain; the difficult climb may be painful, but the joy of reaching the peak is well worth the effort. Don't give up until you get satisfactory results, even if they don't come to you easily!

Left: Four Peony Flowers. *A traditional design on a furoshiki (or Japanese scarf). Executed using the freehand technique.*

Opposite page: *By executing the kasane technique with these two stencil patterns, the author created the design shown on page 78.*

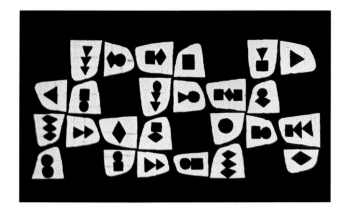

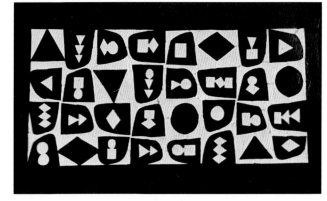

Tsujigahana

This ancient and remarkably sophisticated technique, the aesthetic values of which are still appreciated very highly by the Japanese, was developed during Japan's eighteenth-century Edo era. Either katazome or tsutsugaki is combined with both shibori and fine embroidery (using gold, silver, or shiny silk threads). Traditional kimonos and the ornate costumes used in *Noh* (one of three traditional Japanese theater arts: Kabuki, Bunraku, and Noh) offer breath-taking examples of tsujigahana at its best.

Freehand Drawing (Hand or Spatula)

Designs can be drawn directly on the fabric by hand or with the spatula that is normally used to apply the resist paste in katazome. With this technique, it's important to give free rein to your imagination. Focus on being creative, not on technical perfection. To achieve a truly free-spirited and uninhibited design, imagine yourself painting in a carefree manner on a canvas. Sometimes, the most spontaneously applied designs demonstrate the most charming, unpretentious, and appealing features.

Nazome: Dyeing with Colored Paste (Ironori)

Dyeing with colored paste is a method derived from *surikomi,* rubbing pigments into stencil-covered fabrics by hand. When this is done on fabric with dyes rather than pigments, it is called nazome (textile printing using colored paste instead of printing ink). In nazome, as in silk screening, several pat-

terns are used—as many as there are colors in the design. When applying the paste to paper, use either brushes or spatulas, depending on the type of design. A spatula is more appropriate when you're working with fabric.

To execute this technique, first mix the dye (direct dyes for cellulose fibers, acid dyes for protein fibers, or fiber-reactive dyes for either) according to the instructions given in Chapter Thirteen. Make these solutions about 10% to 20% more concentrated than the regular formulas. Then make the paste, but don't put salt or lime into it; these substances and the dye might counteract each other. Combine the dye and paste; you may need to experiment to find proportions that will yield the results for which you're aiming.

Apply the colored paste, using a different stencil for each color. Instead of washing out the paste after each application, overlap the individual layers of colored paste. Then steam the fabric over boiling water for about 30 minutes to an hour, until the colors have thoroughly settled into the fiber structure. (See Chapter Nine for steaming instructions.)

A variation of nazome, known as *tsutsu-nazome,* involves applying colored paste with the conical tube used in the tsutsugaki technique. This method does save time but doesn't render the same rich yet subtle effects as nazome because the dye doesn't penetrate the fiber as thoroughly. It tends to stay on the fabric's surface instead, resulting in a less appealing look and a lack of impact in both color and aesthetic value.

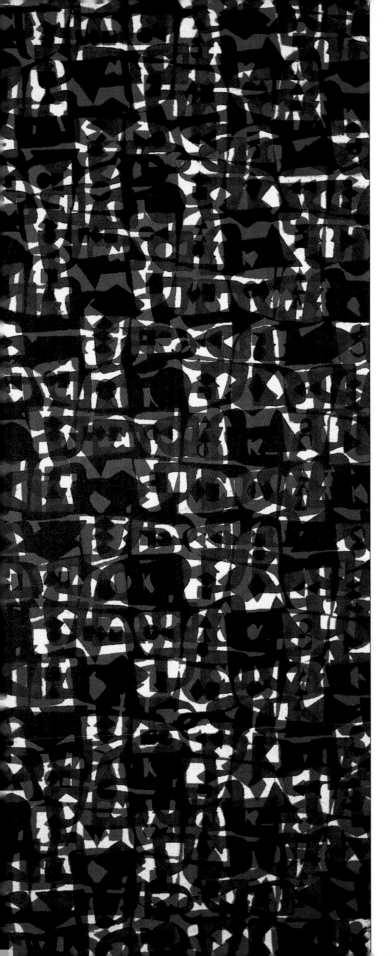

Wood-Block Printing

There are two ways to execute this method; in both of them, the paste is applied with either a carved wooden block or with wooden sticks the ends of which have different shapes. (Don't limit yourself, however, to the use of wood; if you'd like to challenge your creativity, try using found objects—leaves, kitchen utensils, or rocks, for example—as stamps.)

Method One

Select white or very light shades of colored fabric, and use a resist paste that is a little bit softer than that used for regular katazome and tsutsugaki-zome. Apply the paste by stamping it on with the block or with sticks. If you use the latter, try to combine several sticks of different sizes within one design in order to create an interesting effect. Once you've applied paste to the fabric, the rest of the process is the same as that used for katazome. After washing the fabric, the base color will be that of the undyed fabric.

Method Two

White fabrics are most frequently used in this method, but you may work with very light shades of colored fabrics, too. The paste with which the design is stamped is colored (see the "Nazome" section) and is even softer than that used in Method One. Once the paste has been applied, the fabric is steamed. This process settles the colors into the fabric structure, makes them richer and brighter, and ensures their fastness. If you'd like to dye the background as well, you may do so before steaming. After rinsing out the paste, the design will appear in the colors of the dye-and-paste mixture.

Kasane: Overlapping One or More Stencils

Method One

One way of executing this technique is to use exactly the same stencil, creating a single design by repositioning the stencil several times. Partial, irregular, accidental, or well-planned overlapping are all acceptable in the color arrangement of the final design. No matter how you place the stencil, however, you must remove the paste each time you reposition it. If you don't, you'll find it impossible to obtain desirable colors and compositions. You may use various shades of a single hue or multiple hues, shades, and chroma.

Method Two

Another way to execute kasane is to overlap separate stencil patterns. The nature of these patterns can be entirely different: positive and negative patterns, geometric and organic patterns, or white background and solid background patterns can all make fascinating designs. Mixing different stencil patterns in this manner is a technique that originated in Okinawa; it's known as *oboro-gata.* The following instructions for oboro-gata combinations are just two examples of kasane execution.

In this first example, start by applying the paste through a stencil with a positive pattern. Then complete irosashi (detail coloring), fusenori (covering the dyed details with resist paste), and *jizome* (background dyeing). Next, position a negative-pattern stencil that is an exact reverse of the positive pattern, and apply resist paste over it. Dye with a dark color to finish. In this case, mizumoto should be done only once, at the end of the process. For the best effect, the background (or base) color should be a comparatively light shade. The result will be quite exciting; the dark shades of the partially colored areas will convey the feeling of a deep forest or of distant mountains rising beyond lakes.

In this second example of oboro-gata, use a negative pattern first. Complete all the steps of irosashi, and as soon as you're finished, wash out the resist paste from the fabric. Next, attach the fabric to a paste-laying board, and place a komon-type stencil pattern on the fabric. (It's important to use a stencil the cut-out areas of which are relatively small.) Using the conical tube, cover the previously dyed areas with paste, and then dye the background. Finally, wash the tsutsu-applied paste out of the fabric. This method gives the effect of multiple colors, and its unique komon background expresses the features of katazome with unequalled grace and delicacy.

Opposite page: Geometric Composition. *The two complementary stencil patterns shown on page 77 were overlapped to dye this Japanese obi (or belt).*

Right: Sun Flower I. *This stencil-dyed yardage fabric was created by overlapping a single stencil pattern, the one shown on the next page.*

Chusen-Zome: Semi Mass-Produced Repeated Designs

In Japan, this technique is often used for mass production of functional rather than artistic or creative items. In recent years, however, many outstanding craftsmen have realized its aesthetic potential, and chusen is now very popular. It permits one to dye both sides of the fabric simultaneously, to dye a great deal of fabric in relatively few steps, and to achieve speed without sacrificing handmade quality.

First, you'll need to construct a wooden frame and attach your stencil to it. Then, with one or more hinges, attach the frame's top edge to the paste-laying board's top edge. The frame will secure the stencil at the exact place where you wish to apply the paste to the fabric.

Now fold your length of fabric (accordion-style) into equal sections, each comprising a single design unit. Crease the folds, and then unfold the fabric. Next, lift the hinged frame, and place the first section of fabric under it. Lower the frame over the fabric section, and apply paste through the stencil. Lift the frame, and fold the next section of fabric over on top of the paste-covered section. Note that the face of this section will lie directly on top of the section to which you've just applied paste. Lower the frame again, and apply paste to the upper face of the section that you've lowered in place.

Repeat this process until you've applied paste to alternate sections along the whole length of fabric. When you get to the last layer, make sure to put an extra folded section of fabric on top of the last pasted layer to protect its surface. The designs on each layer of paste-covered fabric should match each other exactly.

Place the folded fabric onto a flat, metal-screen frame, and then pour hot dye solution over the fabric before the paste dries out. (Note that in no other paste-resist method can the fabric be dyed while the paste is damp.) Almost any kind of dye will work with this method, but vat dyes are the best choice. Blow air through the fabric when you're through. As soon as you've finished pouring the dye, wash the paste out—another unique aspect of timing in this method.

Opposite page: This contemporary stencil pattern was overlapped to dye the yardage fabric shown on page 79.

Right and below: Designed and executed by Yunoki Samiro, these three pieces were dyed by using the chusen method.

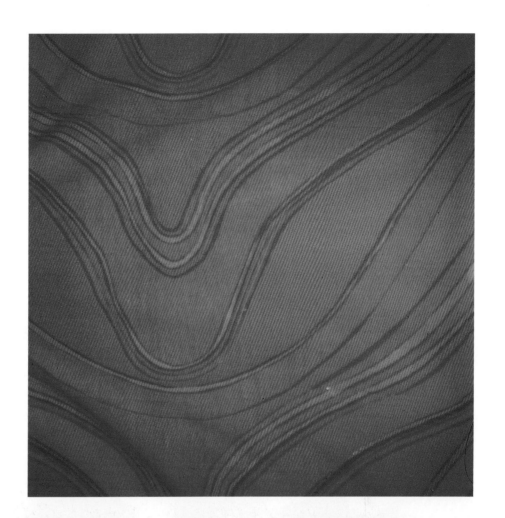

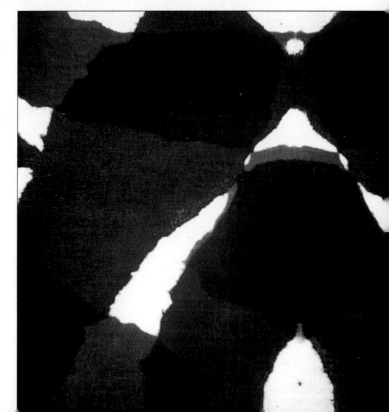

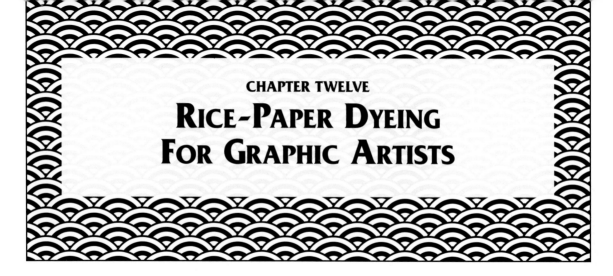

CHAPTER TWELVE
RICE-PAPER DYEING
FOR GRAPHIC ARTISTS

Rice-paper dyeing has its origins in *chiyo-gami* (the decoratively dyed papers with which young Japanese girls used to play) and in the sample pattern papers for *ai-ya* (professional indigo-blue dyers). In modern times, the technique has been developed for many uses, including wallpapers, book covers, gift and note cards, wrapping papers, Christmas cards, fans, and calendars. It is especially recommended for use by graphic artists.

The paper used in this dyeing technique must be strong enough to be washed in water, so that it won't be damaged when you remove the resist paste. Several suitable kinds of rice paper are made in Japan. When purchasing paper in other countries, however, take care not to use the type which, while it may look appropriate, will melt in water! Before you apply the paste, test your paper by soaking a sample sheet in water for 15 minutes.

The process differs somewhat from that used to dye fabric; the paste is mixed differently, soybean juice is not needed for sizing, and the paper isn't stretched on harite or shinshi. You don't need to attach your rice paper to a paste-laying board, either.

The resist paste used on rice paper is similar to that used in a technique known as *kakiotoshi*—a technique originally developed for dyeing leather. Called *itchin-nori,* this paste consists of a mixture of three parts wheat flour to two parts rice bran. Mix the flour and bran thoroughly. Then gradually add hot water (about 25% more than you used to make paste for fabric application), mixing it in carefully to make a paste that is considerably thinner than the one used in katazome. Shape the paste into doughnuts, steam, and mash with slaked lime solution and salt, as explained in Chapter Six. (This same paste can be also be used to execute tsutsugaki on rice paper.)

With thumb tacks, secure the top of the stencil to a wooden table-top or work surface. Next, insert a stack of 30 to 50 sheets of rice paper underneath the pattern, and apply the paste through the stencil, sheet by sheet. Then suspend a clothesline indoors.

Use clothespins to attach the sheets to the line in pairs, with their pasted surfaces facing outward. Because the resist paste is thinner than the one used on fabric, unless the air is especially humid, the paste will dry in about 30 minutes.

Next, apply the pigments, and then hang the sheets again until they're dry. Soak the paper in water for at least 30 minutes, and then wash out the paste, but don't scrub too vigorously. Avoid distorting the paper; just brush the surface lightly with a soft-bristled brush. Rice paper is hardy, but not as strong as fabric, so be careful not to rub its surface too many times, or you'll damage it. Hang the sheets to dry once again. To remove wrinkles, iron the dry paper on its non-colored side with an iron set at a low temperature.

In recent years, a number of Japanese graphic artists and print makers have realized how well stencil dyeing can be adapted for use in print making. Though its features and results are similar to wood-block printing, the process has many advantages over this technique and over silk screening as well. Fine lines and details are more easily achieved with stencils

Opposite page*: Paste-resist dyeing on rice paper provides an aesthetically pleasing and functional alternative to dyeing on fabric.*

Right: Mining. *Shown on this page and on pages 84 and 85 are a series of industrial panels that the author stencil-dyed on rice paper. The works were commissioned by Mitsui & Company.*

than with wood; stencil papers are also more flexible and easier to store than either wood blocks or silk-screening frames. And in stencil dyeing, you need only one pattern, even when you desire multiple colors, whereas wood-block printing and silk screening require a separate block or frame for each color application. In stencil dyeing, the only time you must have more than a single pattern is when you wish to overlap different designs.

Last but not least, unlike wood-block printing and silk screening, stencil dyeing requires no harsh, potentially carcinogenic, chemical agents. Environmental specialists and many school administrators, teachers, students, and artists are familiar with the complaints that arise when people are exposed to harsh chemicals. In fact, so hazardous are some of the chemicals used in silk screening that many distributors will no longer provide these supplies to educational institutions. Stencil dyeing provides an ideal alternative, not only within school curricula but also in the personal studio. The resist paste, which is made of natural ingredients and which requires no chemicals during the washing process, is entirely safe to use.

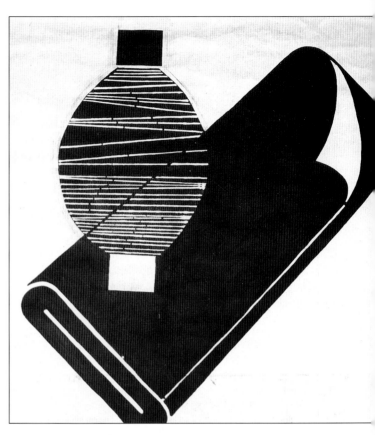

Top: Textiles

Left: Construction

84

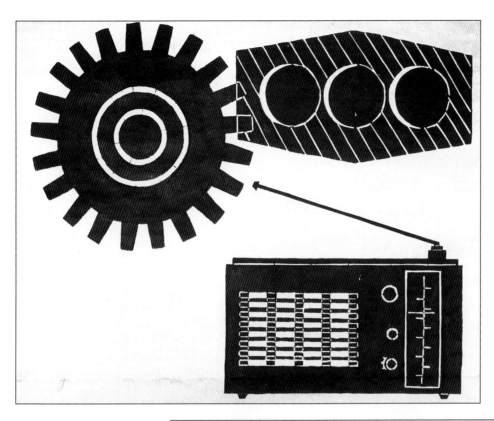

Top: Machinery

Right: Transportation

Left: Menu, papers for fan-making, and calendars, all designed by Keisuke Serizawa and executed on rice paper by anonymous artisans.

Below: Dyed rice paper for fans. Designed by Keisuke Serizawa.

Opposite page, top: Another piece of dyed rice paper for a fan. Designed by Keisuke Serizawa.

Opposite page, bottom: Contemporary abstract design on rice paper, also shown on the book's cover.

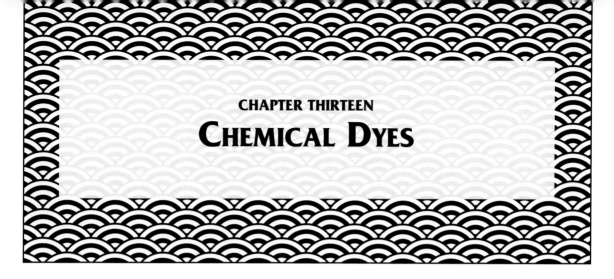

CHEMICAL DYES

Because the focus of this book is on paste-resist methods rather than on dye preparation and application, it would be wise for the beginner to spend some time locating and reading a few of the many books available on chemical dyes. In addition, dyers should actively seek specific information on each dye they use; dyes improve and change from year to year, and similar types of dyes differ slightly depending upon their manufacturer. Most dyes are sold with instructions for preparation and application. Manufacturers and distributors of dyestuffs will often provide specific advice to individual customers. Just give your supplier a call if you have questions.

Only those chemical dyes that can be applied by brush and those that don't require high temperatures for proper application are recommended for stencil dyeing. Among those suitable for katazome are some fiber-reactive dyes (for both cellulose and protein fibers), direct dyes (for cellulose fibers), acid dyes (for protein fibers), and vat dyes. Before you can select an appropriate chemical dye, you'll need to know exactly what kind of fiber and technique you're going to use and whether your project will be functional, decorative, or strictly creative or experimental in concept.

Remember to use clean, non-reactive containers when mixing dyes and when dyeing in a dyebath. Enamel is a good choice.

Fiber-Reactive Dyes

Fiber-reactive dyes, first introduced by Imperial Chemical Industries, Ltd. under the brand name *Procion,* are used primarily with cellulose fibers but can be applied to protein fibers as well. These dyes are ideal for use with paste-resist techniques. They are not water-soluble, they are washfast, and the

dye powders can be stored almost indefinitely. Even though fiber-reactive dyes are time-consuming to apply, don't store well once mixed, and can be relatively expensive, they are excellent for brush-application.

The Procion MX series of dyes are the fiber-reactive dyes most suitable for stencil-dyeing; they need not be hot in order to react with the fiber. Instead, the reaction between dye and fiber takes place in the presence of an alkali and urea. They are most satisfactory for use on natural fibers: viscose rayon, cotton, linen, silk, wool, and any combinations of these fibers.

For Direct Application

Chart II (on page 98) provides a list of ingredients for making Procion MX dye solutions for brush-application on cotton, linen, viscose rayon, wool, and silk. Dyers who wish to mix up to four different colors of dye solution should refer to Chart III (also on page 98), which provides formulas for one cup of stock chemical solution. One cup of this stock solution will be enough for a total of four half-cups of dye liquid (one-half cup of each color). To make two cups of the stock solution, just double the formulas in Chart III. Here are some tips regarding the dye and stock solution formulas:

When you mix dye solutions, the amount of dye powder will vary according to the color and value you wish to obtain.

You may need to adjust the amount of thickener depending upon the absorbency of the fabric to be dyed.

The amount of urea and soda in the dye recipe is increased in proportion to the total amount of liquid used.

Tropical Plant in Red.
Stencil-dyed yardage fabric.

Once the bicarbonate of soda has been added, the dye should be used within 48 hours. After that time period, though the color may look correct as you're applying it, when the fabric is heat-treated and rinsed, the areas you dye with the stale solution will differ in shade from those dyed earlier. If the soda is omitted, the solution can be mixed in advance and will last two to three months if refrigerated.

It's a good idea to keep records of the formulas you use for each dye powder. Chart IV (on page 98) offers a sample record-keeping procedure.

If you're using vinegar instead of acetic acid (see the wool and silk formulas), you will need to reduce the amount of water.

When mixing a stock solution for black (for cellulose fibers), you'll need to reduce the amount of urea. See the recipe for a black dye solution on page 90.

Use only Black 600 for the wool and silk formulas.

Following are instructions for making 1/2 cup (118.3 ml) of a medium-value Procion MX dye solution for cotton (see Chart II). Note that the Ludigol water acts as a stabilizer to keep the dye from oxidizing too quickly. The sodium alginate thickens the dye to keep it from spreading and bleeding.

Both the Ludigol water and thickener should be made the night before you intend to use them. Prepare the thickener by sprinkling two heaping teaspoons (10 g) of sodium alginate over the surface of two cups (473 ml) of room-temperature water. Stir well to dissolve, and allow the mixture to sit for several hours. To make the Ludigol water, dissolve 1-1/4 teaspoons (4 g) of Ludigol into two cups (473 ml) of room-temperature water. (A blender will prove useful here.)

By adding an alkali mix of washing soda (or PRO Dye Activator) and baking soda to your prepared dye solution, you can avoid having to steam the fabric or dry it at a high temperature. Thoroughly mix four parts PRO Dye Activator and one part baking soda, or one part washing soda and eight parts baking soda. Store these mixed powders in a container until you're ready to use them.

To prepare the dye solution (just before you're ready to apply it), dissolve 1/2 teaspoon (approximately 1.5 g) of dye powder in 1/4 cup (59 ml) of Ludigol water. Then add one tablespoon (15 g) of urea and mix. Add 1/2 teaspoon (3.5 g) of bicarbonate of soda and mix again. Add 1/4 cup (59 ml) of thickener and mix. Let the solution sit for 15 minutes before you use it.

The recipe for making black is slightly different. Use three to four teaspoons (8.25 to 11 g) of black dye powder, 1/2 teaspoon (2.5 g) of urea, and two teaspoons (14 g) of bicarbonate of soda.

Just before you're ready to start dyeing, add one teaspoon (4 g) of the mixed alkali to each cup (237 ml) of prepared dye solution. Mix the powder in well. Once it has been added, the dye solution will only last about four hours. If you wish to prolong the useful life of your dye solution, you may omit adding the mixed alkali, but you will then need to heat-set the

dye once it has been applied. Instructions for doing so are provided in the paragraphs that follow.

After the dye has been applied, allow the fabric to air dry for 24 hours, but be sure that the air temperature is at least 70° F (21° C); outdoor drying on a sunny day will work well. If the weather is chilly, however, or if you've omitted the mixed alkali, you must air dry the fabric and then either steam it or place it into a clothes dryer, set at a high temperature, for 30 to 45 minutes, depending on the fabric's thickness and size. Neither steaming nor high-heat drying is recommended for silk, however, so for silk application, be sure to add the mixed alkali to the dye.

Next, wash the paste out by immersing the fabric in a tub of room-temperature water and swishing it around gently. Don't be alarmed by color escaping into the water. Drain and refill the tub, repeating this process until the water comes out almost clear, and all the paste is removed. Black and red sometimes bleed more than other colors, so be sure to rinse the fabric completely when using these colors.

Now fill the tub with hot water. Move the fabric around in this water, draining and refilling the tub until the rinse is clear and until the fabric no longer

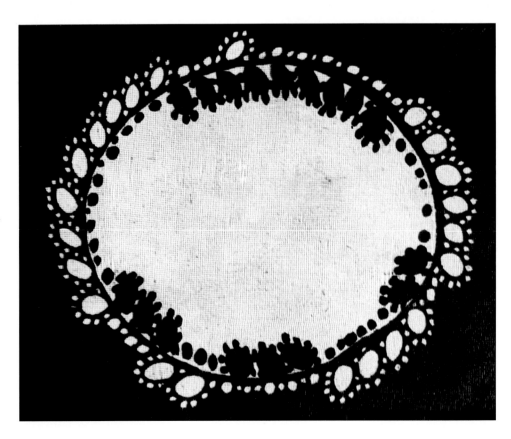

The author used a contemporary abstract stencil pattern (left) and chemical dyes to create the yardage shown on the opposite page.

feels slimy to the touch. (This slimy feel is caused by the thickener). Wash the fabric with Synthrapol or with a mild dish detergent, and complete a final, room-temperature rinse. Allow the fabric to soak in this final rinse in order to help prevent bleeding. Pat the fabric dry with a towel; don't wring it. Then stretch the fabric on harite to dry.

For Dyebath Application

If you wish to dye your fabric by submersion in a dye-bath, the following Procion dye recipe (for one pound or 454.4 g of fabric) will work well.

The fabric to be dyed must be free of dirt, stains, and oily spots, or the dye won't "take" uniformly and completely. Wash the fabric, using a good detergent, in a washing machine set on a hot-water cycle, or by hand, using water that is as hot as possible. Rinse the fabric thoroughly in hot water.

To determine the intensity of the shade you wish to attain on the fabric, use Chart V (on page 99). Sprinkle the desired amount of dye powder into two cups (473.2 ml) of warm water, not over 100° F (38° C), stirring constantly. When the dye has dissolved completely, add this solution to 10.5 quarts (9.93 l or 336 fl. oz.) of room-temperature water. Be sure to use a stainless steel or plastic pail.

Next, stir common salt (in an amount equal to the weight of the fabric) into the water. When the salt has dissolved, add the fabric to the dyebath. Stir the fabric and dyebath intermittently for ten to fifteen minutes. Dissolve four tablespoons (60 g) of washing soda (or PRO Dye Activator) in a small amount of warm water, and add it to the dyebath. Stir constantly for five minutes and then intermittently for 30 to 60 minutes—30 for pale shades and 60 for heavy shades.

Rinse the fabric well in cool water until the water is almost clear. Then wash it in water that is as hot as possible, using a mild detergent. Rinse well again and dry.

Direct Dyes

Direct dyes, which are recommended for cellulose fibers such as cotton, linen, rayon, and jute, are among the easiest dyes to apply. Though they aren't easy to dissolve, once they are dissolved, colors are easily mixed. Their final colors can be identified as soon as the dye has been applied. Direct dyes, however, which are water-soluble, don't stand up excep-

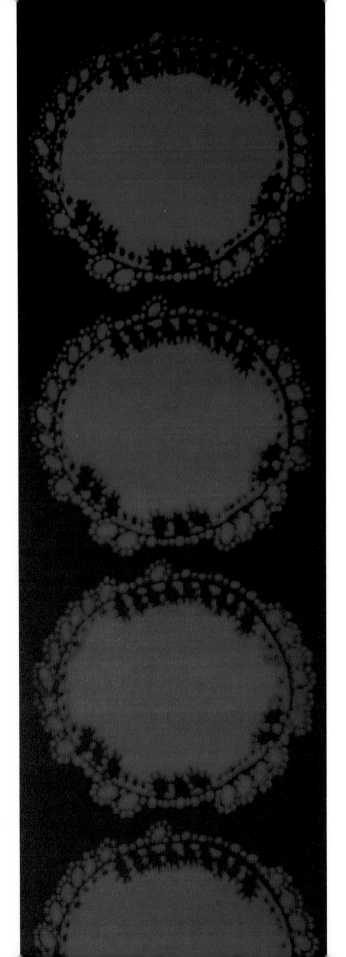

tionally well to repeated washing or to the effects of sunlight. They do require steaming and a dyeing assistant such as washing soda. Recipes often include salt or vinegar as well. Because direct dyes differ slightly, depending upon their manufacturer, you will need to rely on the printed instructions that come with them or on your dye supplier for advice regarding their use.

Purchase major colors (red, yellow, blue, orange, green, and brown) and mix as needed. You can create black by mixing all these colors together. When mixing colors, always make a concentrated solution of each separate color first. Combine and then dilute these stock solutions when you're ready to use them. Store the dye powder in a tight container, as it will absorb humidity easily.

Direct dyes for katazome are generally mixed in a 1% solution (1 gram or .035 oz. of dye per 100 ml or 3.38 fl. oz. of water) and then combined with a 1% washing-soda solution, which serves to settle the color into the fabric. You will probably need to adjust the amount of washing soda, as the dye will settle differently on different fabrics. For lighter or darker shades, reduce or increase the amount of dyestuff by 20% to 30%.

Begin by pasting the powdered dye with a little hot water or alcohol. Then create a concentrated stock solution by adding a small amount of boiling water and simmering the concentrated solution until all the dye has dissolved. Store the stock solution in a tight, non-reactive container. When you're ready to use the solution, first add half the required amount of boiling water (to make a 1% solution) to it. Then mix the other half of the boiling water with the washing soda. Finally add the washing-soda solution to the dye solution. (Always test your solution on a scrap of fabric before starting.) Solutions may be stored by heating them briefly and placing them in the refrigerator, though they won't last more than two or three days.

Direct dyes are applied in a similar manner to pigments. First apply the resist paste and soybean-juice sizing. Then brush on the dye, using repeated thin coats rather than a single thick coat. To achieve even coloring, use stencil brushes to rub the dye into the fiber structure as thoroughly as possible. For intense colors, apply three coats rather than two. Remember that it's very important to let each coat dry before you apply the next.

If you are vat-dyeing, soak the fabric for only three-quarters as long as you would soak it if you were

using pigments. Dyes are more likely than pigments to creep under the resist paste. When too much dye is applied, it will bleed into the water as you wash the paste from the fabric and will return to the now unprotected fabric.

Acid Dyes

Acid dyes (recommended only for protein fibers such as silk and wool) are brighter in color than direct dyes, are easy to apply, less expensive than fiber-reactive dyes, and develop their colors quickly. They're prepared, stored, and applied much as direct dyes are. These water-soluble dyes have disadvantages, too: they're less washfast than fiber-reactive dyes, and they do require steaming. Within the acid dye family are the 1:2 pre-metallized dyes, which withstand the effects of washing and exposure to sunlight better than ordinary acid dyes.

Neither direct dyes nor acid dyes are entirely permanent under normal cleaning and washing conditions; they should be dry-cleaned.

Vat Dyes

Vat dyes are made water-soluble by treating them with a reducing agent, a chemical that removes the oxygen in them. In their reduced form, they can be dissolved in water that is alkaline. When the dyed fabric is exposed to air, the dye is oxidized and becomes water-insoluble once again. Because the color of the dye solution is different from the final color of the oxidized dye on the fabric, it's difficult to judge color values and shades as the dye is applied.

These dyes, which have a direct affinity for cellulose fibers but which can be used with wool and silk if an assisting agent is added, are exceptionally fast and do not require steaming. Their colors are generally fairly light in shade and clear and soft in appearance. Their most serious disadvantages are that they are time-consuming to prepare and apply and are somewhat dangerous to handle. The beginner should not work with vat dyes unless an experienced dyer is present. Dye recipes are available from the manufacturers of these dyes and can be found in books on vat dyeing.

After Dyeing

After dyeing, steam the fabric if necessary. Then wash the resist paste from the fabric, making sure that all the residual dye is removed, too. When using chemical dyes, it's especially important to rinse the fabric until the water is clear. Suspend the fabric on harite to dry; the horizontal drying position will ensure that colors are distributed evenly.

If a final fixer is required, soak the fabric for 15 to 20 minutes in a mixture of three grams of fixer to one liter of water (or 1/2 oz. per gallon), and then allow it to dry. Then rinse the fixer out thoroughly, stretch the fabric on harite, and dry it in sunlight once again. Avoid wringing the fabric at any stage; wringing will create wrinkles.

Opposite page:
Sun Flower II. *Stencil-dyed wall-hanging. Note that the same stencil pattern was used to create the rice-paper design shown on page 87 and on the book's cover.*

Right: *Stencil-dyed rice paper, designed and executed by the author.*

GALLERY

The Japanese artists whose works are shown in this gallery are among the finest in the contemporary world of dyeing. All pieces are stencil-dyed.

Opposite page: Rain
Syojiro Kato
1991
5' 11" x 4' 8" (180 x 142 cm)
Acid dye on silk (a folding screen)
Photo by Seiryukai

Right: '91 Design of Flying
Mihoko Ogino
1991
6' 7" x 6' 7" (200 x 200 cm)
Vegetable dye on cotton
Photo by Seiryukai

Below: Mountscape
Hideharu Naito
1991
5' 9" x 16' 9" (175 x 510 cm)
Natural indigo on hemp

Above: Suddenly-91-2
Yukihiko Tajima
1991
17-1/3" x 25-1/5" (44 x 64 cm)
Pigment on bamboo paper
Photo by Seiryukai

Left: Decision
Keiko Kanesaki
1990
6' 7" x 4' 5" (200 x 135 cm)
Fiber-reactive dye on cotton

CHART I
NATURAL DYES

DYE	MORDANT	COLOR RANGE	SUITABLE FIBER	COLOR FASTNESS
Indigo (1)	Alum	Blues	All natural fibers except linen	Excellent
Indigo (2)	Chrome	Greens	Wool and silk	Good
Gum catechu (Cutch)	Alum	Browns	All natural fibers	Excellent
	None	Rusts	All natural fibers	Excellent
	Copperas	Dark browns or	All natural fibers	Excellent
		Greys and blacks	Some wools and vegetable fibers	Excellent
Peach leaves	Alum	Yellows	Wool and silk	Good
Logwood	None	Blues	Wool	Fair to good
	Chrome	Dark blues	Silk	Good
	Chrome	Black	Wool	Good
	Alum	Dark purples	All natural fibers	Good
	Copperas	Dark blues and blacks	Wool	Good
Madder roots	Alum	Reds	All natural fibers	Excellent
	Chrome	Oranges and rusts	All natural fibers	Excellent
Mullein	Alum	Yellows	All natural fibers	Excellent
	Chrome	Golds	All natural fibers	Excellent
	Tin	Bright yellows	All natural fibers	Excellent
Queen Anne's Lace	Alum	Pale yellows	All natural fibers	Good
	Chrome	Tans	All natural fibers	Good
Cudbear	Alum	Reds	All natural fibers	Excellent
	Tin	Purples	All natural fibers	Excellent
Alkanet roots	None	Gray-blues	Wool	Good
	Acetic acid	Red-purple and browns	Wool	Good
	Alum	Red-tans	All natural fibers	Fair to good
Turmeric	Alum	·Yellows	All natural fibers	Fair to good
	Chrome	Golds and brasses	All natural fibers	Fair to good
Coffee	Alum	Tans	All natural fibers	Good

Chart II
Formulas for 1/2 Cup (118.3 ml)
of Liquid Procion MX Fiber-Reactive Dye

Ingredients	For Cotton, Linen, and Viscose Rayon	For Wool	For Silk
Ludigol Water	1/4 cup (59.15 ml)	1/4 cup (59.15 ml)	1/4 cup (59.15 ml)
Urea	1 to 2 tbsp. (15 g to 30 g)	2 tbsp. (30 g)	2-1/2 tbsp. (37.5 g)
Bicarbonate of Soda	1/2 tsp. (3.5 g)	——————	——————
Acetic Acid (56%) or	——————	1/4 tsp. (1.25 ml) or	1/4 tsp. (1.25 ml) or
Vinegar	——————	5-1/2 tsp. (27.5 ml)	5-1/2 tsp. (27.5 ml)
Synthrapol	——————	1/8 tsp. (.63 ml)	1/8 tsp. (.63 ml)
Wool Assistant	——————	1/4 tsp. (1.6 g.)	——————
Thickener (sodium alginate)	1/4 cup (59.15 ml)	1/4 cup (59.15 ml)	1/4 cup (59.15 ml)

Chart III
Formulas for One Cup of Stock Chemical Solution

Ingredient	Cellulose Fibers (Cotton, Linen, and Viscose Rayon)	Protein Fibers (Wool and Silk)	
Room-temperature water	1 cup (237 ml)	1 cup (237 ml)	1 cup (237 ml)
Ludigol	3/4 tsp. (2.4 g)	3/4 tsp. (2.4 g)	3/4 tsp. (2.4 g)
Urea	4 tbsp. (60 g)	8 tbsp. (120 g)	10 tbsp. (150 g)
Acetic Acid or	——————	1 tsp. (5 ml) or	1 tsp. (5 ml) or
Vinegar	——————	22 tsp. (110 ml)	22 tsp. (110 ml)
Synthrapol	——————	1/4 tsp. (1.3 ml)	1/4 tsp. (1.3 ml)
Wool Assistant	——————	1 tsp. (6.4 ml)	——————
Bicarbonate of Soda	1 tsp. (7 g)	——————	——————

Chart IV
Samples of Record-Keeping for Dye Formulas

Color	Water	Urea	Bicarbonate of Soda	Thickener
1/2 cup (118.3 ml) Medium Yellow: 1/2 tsp. (1.35 g) Yellow Dye Powder	1/4 cup (59.2 ml)	1 tbsp. (15 g)	1/2 tsp. (3.5 g)	1/4 cup (59.2 ml)
1/2 cup (118.3 ml) Cool Gray: 1 tsp. (3 g) Black Dye Powder	1/4 cup (59.2 ml)	1/2 tsp. (2.5 g)	2 tsp. (14 g)	1/4 cup (59.2 ml)
1/2 cup (118.3 ml) Dark Green: 1 tsp. (2.7 g) Yellow Dye Powder 1/2 tsp. (1.5 g) Blue Dye Powder 1/2 tsp. (1.5 g) Black Dye Powder	1/4 cup (59.2 ml)	1 tbsp. (15 g)	1/2 tsp. (3.5 g)	1/4 cup (59.2 ml)

CHART V
AMOUNT OF DYE PER POUND
(454.4 G) OF FABRIC
FOR LONG DYEBATH

SHADE	GRAMS	TEASPOONS
Pale	3	1
Medium	9	3
Heavy	18	6

DYE CLASSIFICATIONS

ACID DYES

The term applies to the method of application. These dyes are applied to protein fibers (silk and wool); they attach to the fiber through an acid-base reaction and electrolytic attraction.

AZOIC DYES

Naphthol dyes were developed in Germany in 1912. They are very washfast but have been discontinued because beta napthol is a proven carcinogen. They are also difficult to apply.

BASIC DYES

These are used on silk and wool, and on cotton when used with a mordant. They have brilliant colors but poor lightfastness and only moderate washfastness. (They have excellent light and washfastness when applied on acrylic fibers.) In recent years, flourescent colors have been obtained with these dyes. You'll need good ventilation when working with basic dyes, because the solvent methanol has highly toxic fumes.

DIRECT DYES

Direct dyes have a strong affinity for cellulose fibers (cotton, linen, and rayon) and are the simplest means of coloring them. They are not especially washfast, but they are fast when dry-cleaned. The chemical fixative most often used with direct dyes is formaldehyde, which is a suspected carcinogen.

DISPERSE DYES

These dyes were developed for acetate rayon (the first true synthetic). They dye polyester and triacetate very levelly. Disperse dyes are water insoluble. The dye dissolves into the fiber through potentially carcinogenic carriers.

MORDANT DYES

Since ancient times, these dyes have been made by extracting synthetic colors from natural, organic materials. The dyestuff's affinity with the fiber occurs through the use of a mordant. Most of the mordants used are heavy metals, which can be toxic. When they are disposed of carelessly, mordants can cause problems with water systems such as wells and with wildlife and soil . Mordant dyes range in color value but do not provide very bright colors.

PIGMENTS

Pigments and fabric paints are synonymous. The color particles are dispersed, more or less evenly, through a medium or binder. Pigments are not water-soluble.

REACTIVE DYES

These dyes, which react chemically with the fiber, were developed by ICI Industries, and have replaced direct and naphthol dyes in the industry. They have good color and washfastness.

SULFUR DYES

These are used in the dyeing of denims. The insoluble chemical is reduced, applied to the fiber, and then oxidized. They're easy to apply, but they're not fast to bleaching and do not have great color penetration.

VAT DYES

Vat dyes are close relatives to sulfur dyes and are very washfast but are difficult to use and to store. Indigo is a form of vat dye; it does not penetrate the fiber.

BIBLIOGRAPHY

Albers, Anni. *On Designing.* New Haven: Pellango Press, 1959.

Birrell, Vera Leone. *The Textile Arts: A Handbook of Weaving, Braiding, Printing, and Other Textile Techniques.* New York: Schocken Books, 1973.

Conley, Emma. *Vegetable Dyeing.* 2d ed. Penland, North Carolina: Penland School of Crafts, n.d.

Davidson, Mary Frances. *The Dye-Pot.* Middlesboro, Kentucky: Shuttlecraft Shop, 1950.

Hartung, Rolf. *Creative Textile Design: Thread and Fabric.* Translated by Brian Battershaw. New York: Reinhold Pub. Corp., 1964.

Hickethier, Alfred. *Color Mixing by Numbers.* Translated by F. Bradley. New York: Van Nostrand Reinhold Co., 1970.

Johnston, Meda Parker, and Glen Kaufman. *Design on Fabrics.* New York: Van Nostrand Reinhold, 1977.

—- *Design on Fabrics.* 2d ed. New York: Van Nostrand Reinhold Co., 1981.

Keller, Ila. *Batik: The Art and Craft.* Rutland, VT: C.E. Tuttle Co., 1966.

Kierstead, Sallie Pease. *Natural Dyes.* Boston: Humphries, 1950.

Knutson, Linda. *Synthetic Dyes for Natural Fibers.* Rev. ed. Seattle: Madrona Publishers, 1986.

Krevitsky, Nik. *Batik Art and Craft.* New York, Reinhold Pub. Corp., 1964.

Langewis, Laurens, and Frits A. Wagner. *Decorative Art in Indonesian Textiles.* Amsterdam: C.P.J. van der Peet, 1964.

Leggett, William Ferguson. *Ancient and Medieval Dyes.* Brooklyn: Chemical Pub. Co., 1944.

Lesch, Alma. *Vegetable Dyeing: 151 Color Recipes for Dyeing Yarns and Fabrics with Natural Materials.* New York: Watson-Guptill Publications, 1970.

Liles, J. N. *The Art and Craft of Natural Dyeing: Traditional Recipes for Modern Use.* Knoxville: The University of Tennessee Press, 1990.

Maile, Anne. *Tie and Dye as a Present Day Craft.* New York: Taplinger Pub. Co., 1970.

Mairet, Ethel M. *Vegetable Dyes: Being a Book of Recipes and Other Information Useful to the Dyer.* London: Faber and Faber, 1952.

Mattil, Edward L. *Meaning in Crafts.* 3d ed. Englewood Cliffs, NJ: Prentice-Hall, 1971.

Mijer, Pieter. *Batiks, and How to Make Them.* 7th ed. New York: Dodd, Mead, 1925.

Muhling, Ernest. *The Book of Batik.* New York: Taplinger Pub. Co., 1967.

Russ, Stephen. *Fabric Printing by Hand.* New York: Watson-Guptill Publications, 1965.

Samuel, Evelyn. *Introducing Batik.* New York: Watson-Guptill Publications, 1968.

Schwalbach, Mathilda V., and James A Schwalbach. *Screen-Process Printing for the Serigrapher and Textile Designer.* New York: Van Nostrand Reinhold Co., 1970.

Strache, *Wolf. Forms & Patterns in Nature.* New York: Pantheon Books, Inc., 1973.

Glossary

Ai-ya. Professional indigo-blue dyers.

Alum. A fixing agent for pigments bound with soybean juice, as well as a mordant for natural dyes.

Aizome. Processing and fermenting the indigo plant; dyeing with indigo.

Atosashi. The "final touch." Refining detail colors or embellishing the entire design area by applying transparent pigment or dye.

Bero. Transparent, Prussian-blue pigment.

Bingata-zome (bingata). Okinawan style of kata-zome characterized by bright colors (often reds) and by butterflies, flowers, and pine trees which are always featured along with clouds or water.

Catechu (or **cutch**). A vegetable dye derived from juice extracted from the tree trunk.

Calcium hydroxide. Powdered or crystallized slaked lime.

Chaya-zome. Paste-resist style historically popular among the common people.

Chiyo-gami. Decoratively dyed papers with which Japanese girls used to play.

Chugara. Medium-sized pattern used on bedding fabric.

Chusen-zome. A production system in which dye is poured through pasted, folded fabric to achieve multiple repeats of a single pattern.

Copperas. Iron mordant.

Eba. Traditional design style, characterized by an asymmetrical, irregular, and unrestricted design which is large and is not repeated. Frequently consists of a landscape or flower.

Formalin. A fixative used when both pigment and dye have been applied to the same piece of fabric.

Fuchiba. Uncut border around the carved stencil. Used to keep paste from spreading beyond the design area.

Fusenori. Protecting previously dyed areas with paste in order to achieve specific aesthetic features.

Gofun. An opaque white pigment.

Gradation coloring. Adding shading and accents to partially colored design areas.

Grey goods. Fabrics (plain white or off-white) that come straight from the factory. Usually need scouring.

Hera. Spatula with which resist paste is applied.

Harite. A pair of wooden stretchers used to suspend and stretch fabric lengthwise.

Hinata. Negative designs. Background is colored and figures are not.

Hinata-no-kukuri. Outlined positive designs. Colored figures are surrounded by undyed outlines.

Ichiban-go. The first of two different strengths of juice extracted from soybeans to make the sizing and binder. Thicker and stronger than the second extraction (see Niban-go).

Irodome. Fixing pigment and dye to prevent bleeding.

Ironori. Colored paste, created by adding dye to the paste.

Irosashi. Partial coloring of small portions of the design area.

Itchin-nori. Resist paste used in both kakiotoshi (leather dyeing) and on rice paper.

Jizome. Dyeing the background (or base) colors.

Kaeshi-gata. Method of combining katazome and tsutsugaki-zome.

Kage. Positive designs, in which the figures are colored and the background is not.

Kage-no-kukuri. Outlined negative designs, in which undyed figures are surrounded by dyed outlines.

Kakiotoshi. Leather dyeing.

Karakusa. Traditional design style consisting of arabesque designs (swirling, curved lines and/or floral designs). Frequently used on indigo-dyed bedding and on furosinki (a type of carry-all used to wrap and to carry gifts or personal belongings).

Karu-nori. Resist paste in which flour and bran are mixed in ordinary proportions.

Kasane. Overlapping one or more stencil patterns.

Katagami. Stencil paper.

Kataita. Paste-laying board.

Katazome. Paste-resist stencil dyeing.

Kenro-zome. Durable dyeing with fiber-reactive, naphthol, or soluble vat dyes.

Komon. Traditional design style consisting of small, repeated patterns in relatively tight and closely knit motifs.

Komon-nuka. Fine-grained sweet-rice bran, used for centuries in Japan to execute katazome and yuzen-zome.

Kuinori (sick paste). Resist paste that doesn't work properly because it has molded or spoiled.

Ludigol. An oxidizing agent.

Minogami. Japanese tracing paper.

Mizumoto. Washing the resist paste from the fabric.

Mochiko. Sweet-rice flour used to make the resist paste for katazome.

Mordants. Substances that cause dyes to bond with fiber.

Mushi-nori. Steamed resist paste.

Naku. The situation in which dye bleeds into water as resist paste is removed, causing undesirable stains around designs or on the background area.

Naoshi-bake. Short, wide, absorbent brush used to apply soybean-juice sizing and to finish or correct faults.

Nazome. Dyeing with colored paste (or ironori).

Nebai-nori (sticky paste). Resist paste with a high proportion of sweet-rice flour (mochiko). Contains approximately 50-60% flour and 50-40% sweet-rice bran. Used for fine-lined designs.

Neru. Refining fabric by scouring in a chemical solution.

Niban-go. The second of two different strengths of juice extracted from soybeans to make sizing and binder. Thinner and weaker than the first extraction (see Ichiban-go).

Noh. One of three, traditional Japanese theater arts.

Nori. Resist paste.

Oboro-gata. A traditional Okinawan method of executing kasane by combining several different patterns to create a single design.

Registration marks. Small marks cut on the stencil-paper pattern's four corners to help the dyer to realign the stencil when repeating designs.

Roketsu-zome. Batik (or wax-resist dyeing technique).

Sakui-nori (see Karu-nori)

Sashi-bake (or so-sashi). The brushes used to execute sashi-wake.

Sashi-wake. Filling in all paste-free areas with multiple colors.

Scouring. Pre-treatment of fabric prior to dyeing.

Sekidashi. Tsutsugaki-zome style in which many colors are used.

Shibori-zome (shibori). Tie-dyeing.

Shinshi. Fabric stretchers made from flexible bamboo sticks with pins at their ends. The pins pierce the fabric's selvage, stretching the fabric across its width.

Shita-e. Drawing the pattern before carving the stencil paper.

Sizing. Coating the fabric with soybean juice prior to pigment or dye application in order to prevent color bleeding around the design or on the background.

Sodium alginate. Dye thickener that makes it possible to paint or print with dyes.

Suribachi. Japanese earthenware mortar.

Surikomi. Stencil-dyeing technique in which pigments are rubbed into the fabric by hand.

Synthrapol. A non-ionic detergent.

Tsunagi. Stencil-paper joints that serve to hold floating design elements together before gauze has been affixed to the stencil paper.

Tsutsu. Conical tube with which tsutsugaki-zome resist paste is applied.

Tsutsu-nazome. Tsutsugaki-zome executed using colored paste.

Tsutsugaki-zome. Paste-resist variation in which resist-paste is applied freehand through a conical tube (or tsutsu). Also known as tsutsu, noribiki, norigaki, and tenori.

Tsujigahana. Sophisticated combination of katazome or tsutsugaki-zome with both tie-dye and fine embroidery. Developed during the Edo era (seventeenth to eighteenth century).

Yuzen. Traditional technique which combines handpainting with fine lines of tsutsu-applied resist paste. Traditionally created for the aristocracy.

Supply Sources

The sources listed below are only a few of the many that carry dyes and dye-related supplies and equipment. For complete and up-to-date information from any supplier, always request a current catalogue. And don't forget your local craft shops; they may carry what you need or be able to refer you to other sources in your area.

Aiko's Art Materials
3347 North Clark Street
Chicago, IL 60657
Tel: (312) 404-5600
Paste-resist and shibori dyeing supplies, direct dyes, and acid dyes

Horikoshi
55 West 39th Street
18th Floor
New York, NY 10018
Tel: (212) 354-0133
White silk scarves (by the dozen)

Kasuri Dyeworks
1959 Shattuck Avenue
Berkeley, CA 94704
Tel: (510) 841-4509
Paste-resist dyeing supplies, dye textiles, synthetic and natural indigo, and pigments

PRO Chemical & Dye, Inc.
P.O. Box 14
Somerset, MA 02726
Tel: (508) 676-3838
Fax: (508) 676-3980
Orders only: 1-800-BUY-DYE
Fiber-reactive dyes, direct dyes, acid dyes, pigments, dyeing supplies, and chemicals

Testfabrics, Inc.
P.O. Box 420
Middlesex, NJ 08846
Tel: (908) 469-6446
Fax: (908) 469-1147
Dye textiles

Textile Colors
P.O. Box 887
Riverdale, Md. 20738
Tel: 1-800-783-9265
Pigments, direct and acid dyes, dyeing supplies, and chemicals

Conversion of Weights, Measures, and Temperatures

Liquids	U.S.Metric	British
1 fluid ounce (2 tbsp.)	29.6 ml	1.04 fl. oz.
1 pint (16 fl. oz.)	473 ml	16.64 fl. oz.
1 quart (32 fl. oz.)	946 ml	33.28 fl. oz.
1.057 qt. (33.8 fl. oz.)	1 l	35.18 fl. oz.
1 gallon (128 fl. oz.)	3.785 l	133.12 fl. oz.
1 teaspoon	5 ml	
1 tablespoon	15 ml	
1/2 cup	118.3 ml	

Weights	
0.035 oz.	1 gram
1 oz.	28.4 gram
1 cc water (or 1 ml or .034 fl. oz.)	1 gram

Temperatures

To convert Celsius to Fahrenheit: Multiply by 9, divide by 5, and add 32.

To convert Fahrenheit to Celsius: Subtract 32, multiply by 5, and divide by 9.

Linear Measurements

U.S. Inches	Metric CM	U.S. Inches	Metric CM	U.S. Inches	Metric CM
1/8	0.3	9	22.9	30	76.2
1/4	0.6	10	25.4	31	78.7
3/8	1.0	11	27.9	32	81.3
1/2	1.3	12	30.5	33	83.8
5/8	1.6	13	33.0	34	86.4
3/4	1.9	14	35.6	35	88.9
7/8	2.2	15	38.1	36	91.4
1	2.5	16	40.6	37	94.0
1-1/4	3.2	17	43.2	38	96.5
1-1/2	3.8	18	45.7	39	99.1
1-3/4	4.4	19	48.3	40	101.6
2	5.1	20	50.8	41	104.1
2-1/2	6.4	21	53.3	42	106.7
3	7.6	22	55.9	43	109.2
3-1/2	8.9	23	58.4	44	111.8
4	10.2	24	61.0	45	114.3
4-1/2	11.4	25	63.5	46	116.8
5	12.7	26	66.0	47	119.4
6	15.2	27	68.6	48	121.9
7	17.8	28	71.1	49	124.5
8	20.3	29	73.7	50	127.0

INDEX